The Making Of

Led Zeppelin's

(Updated Edition)

By
Robert Godwin

The Making Of Led Zeppelin's ✎ ⚱ ☯ ① (2008 Edition)
by Robert Godwin
© 2008 Robert Godwin Box 62034 Burlington Ontario Canada
ISBN 978-1-894959-90-2

Front Cover photo courtesy Rephoto - Barrie Wentzell
Back cover photo - Dayne Markham
Manufactured in Canada

CONTENTS

FOUR SYMBOLS

No book about Led Zeppelin's fourth album would be complete without an explanation of the cryptic title. The band's third album had been released several months before recording began for the fourth album and had been unmercifully panned by many in the world's music press. The main criticism seems to have been because the album was a significant departure from the first two records. It had included many new styles, including several "acoustic" tracks. Although Zeppelin had used acoustical instruments to good effect on the first and second albums, the third album was dominated by tracks that didn't fit the niche that the media had defined for them. Led Zeppelin were accused of "going soft", and many journalists also accused the band of being "..a hype..".

At this point Page, Plant, Jones and Bonham had worked hard for their recognition. They had toured relentlessly (over 220 shows in 24 months with many double headers) and they believed the accusation of hype was an unjust criticism.

At one point the band were contemplating various different ways to avoid taking the obvious course of calling the next record "Led Zeppelin IV". The release had originally been slated for spring of 1971, at about that time Page commented, *"It might be called Zeppelin IV. Everybody expects that, but we might change it. We've got all sorts of mad ideas. I was thinking at one time of having four EPs, but we want to keep the price down and frankly the price of records now is extortionate."*

Around the same time Robert Plant suggested, *"The intention was for a double album and then we thought "Well, not this time" but then we've been saying "Not this time" since the second album."*

Finally, in an effort to fire a volley back at the press, the decision was made to let the music speak for itself.

Page: *"We decided that on the fourth album we would deliberately play down the group name, and there wouldn't be any information whatsoever on the outer jacket."*

This decision was unprecedented at the time and invoked howls of protest from the band's record label, Atlantic records. Not only was the cover to have no immediately identifiable title, but it would carry none of the other familiar trappings of an album jacket, such as company logos, catalogue numbers, track listings, or most significantly the band's name.

Page: *"Names, titles and things like that don't mean a thing. What does Led Zeppelin* *mean? It doesn't mean a thing. What matters is our music. If we weren't playing good music, nobody would care what we call ourselves. If the music was good, we could call ourselves Cabbages and still get across to our audience."*

Plant: *"We wanted a cover with no writing on it. No company symbols or anything. The hierarchy of the record business aren't into the fact that covers are important to a band's image. We just said they couldn't have the master tapes until they got the cover right."*

When the album finally hit the store shelves (on **November 8th 1971** in the USA and **November 19th** in the UK) the now familiar cover of the derelict house with the picture of an old man carrying sticks on his back provoked an assortment of conflicting reactions from the retailers, the media and the fans. In the first few days frustrated merchants could be seen pulling records out of jackets to see if they had the right album for the customer. Even the dust jacket had no mention of the band; although it did include the production credits mentioning Jimmy Page and Peter Grant. The only other text to be seen were the track titles, a performance credit for Sandy Denny, recording venues, the lyrics to one of the songs (Stairway To Heaven) and most significantly four cryptic symbols.

Because the band had deliberately not given the album a name, the four symbols became the prime candidates to be the title of the record. Although Atlantic went to the trouble of sending artwork copy of the four symbols out to the media, much of the press couldn't be bothered to reproduce them. The obvious result of this was that the album was almost immediately dubbed **"Led Zeppelin IV"**. In later years it was referred to as "The Suicide album" due to Atlantic's belief that it was going to be a commercial flop, but more often it was called ZOSO because the first in the string of four symbols bore some resemblance to the four letters Z O S O. The symbols were also repeated on the label of the record itself and thus aficionados maintained that the symbols *were* the title, which inevitably led to the album being called "Four Symbols".

The exact meaning of the symbols has been the subject of conjecture for years. **Page:** *"Mine was something which I designed myself. A lot of people mistook it for a word - "Zoso" - and many people in the States still refer to the album as "Zoso" which is a pity because it wasn't supposed to be a word at all but something entirely different. Basically the title thing was just another ruse to throw the media into chaos. We all had a good laugh when the record went into the charts and they had to reproduce the symbols instead of a conventional title."*

Since the appearance of the album, critics and fans alike have endeavored to unravel the mysteries of the four symbols. Anyone who delves deeply enough soon realises that symbology is far from an exact science, and the only real constant is that the interpretation is usually wrong.

The four symbols chosen by Led Zeppelin seem to have things in common with each other and with many diverse disciplines. It is almost impossible to divine the intended meaning without the cooperation of the individual who has chosen the symbol. It is, however, extremely easy to go far beyond the intended meaning and exhume all manner of bizarre coincidences and synchronicities. While delving into these particular four symbols the researcher is led from Greek philosophers to ancient Egyptian brotherhoods and Viking mythology, from sunken continents, to 19th century charlatans and mystics. Knowing exactly when to stop looking is virtually impossible.

Page is undoubtedly well read on the various related subjects of symbology and the occult. At one point he owned a book shop in Kensington

The logo for Page's bookshop and Crowley's periodical.

Fig. 1

called **The Equinox** (also the name of a publication by Aleister Crowley) which he had opened to guarantee himself a steady supply of rare books on the subject. As he is not likely to come forward any time soon with an explanation, the following is purely conjecture and the reader is left to interpret it any way they please.

There have been many lengthy dissertations published attempting to explain Page's symbol (Fig. 1), often putting bits and pieces together from astrology or magic texts. Since the last edition of this book Zep collector Duncan Watson and Joseph Peterson of esotericarchives.com discovered that Page's symbol appeared in almost identical form in a book called *The Triple Vocabulary Infernal Manual of Demonography or The Ruses of Hell Uncovered* by Frinellan, published in Paris in 1844. There can be little doubt that this is Page's symbol in the last line (Fig. 2). Frinellan's book confirms various earlier sources including **The True Red Dragon,** (as mentioned in the last edition of this book).

An 1850 reprint of *The True Red Dragon,* published in Paris, claims it was reproduced from a 1521 edition. Page's symbol is part of a sequence that represented Saturn (Saturday) (Fig.2a).

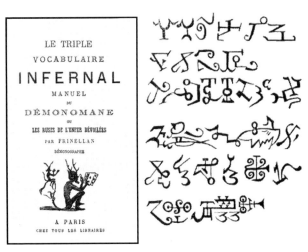

Fig. 2

Fig. 2a

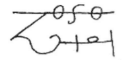

Fig. 2b

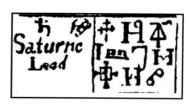

Fig. 2c

Watson and Robert Ansell found another version of a similar symbol from 1557 that appeared in a book *Ars Magica Arteficii (The Magical Art of Artephius)* by G. Cardano, (Fig.2b). This one also represented the planet Saturn, which is frequently associated with Capricorn, Page's birth sign.

Fig. 3

Fig. 4

Interestingly the symbol for Saturn is also the symbol used for **Lead** as seen here in a 17th century manuscript. (Fig. 2c)

Fig. 5

In another early cryptic Zeppelin reference there is a mention of alchemical symbols, specifically to the ancient material "**Electrum**". Electrum was the name used by alchemists to describe a naturally occurring alloy of gold and silver. *Artephius* is believed to have been an alchemist who lived before the 13th century and pursued the elixir of life through alchemy.

Then there was a comment from Page in which he mentioned "**Thursday**" to an interviewer as an explanation. This may have been a spurious diversion by Page, since his symbol seems more closely linked to Saturday.

However, although **Electrum** and **Thursday** seem to be two disparate and totally unconnected references, in fact they both share a common symbol (Fig. 3).

Ancient researchers used the same symbols to refer to metals, planets and deities. This particular symbol was also used to describe Jupiter (both the planet and the Roman god). **Thursday** came from the early Germanic reference to **Thor,** The Defender Of The World (Thor's day). References to Thor in ancient Icelandic literature as the wielder of "The Hammer" are pervasive. Moreover, Thor is sometimes analogous in the Roman pantheon with Jupiter.

Another connection is made through one of the world's oldest surviving alchemical texts the *Codex Marcianus Graecus,* which is on display at St Mark's in Venice. The *Codex* symbol for Jupiter/Thor (Fig. 4) is similar to two different components of Page's symbol . Page's astrological birth sign, **Capricorn** (Fig. 5) is also sometimes associated with Jupiter and Thursday.

Jupiter's bolt of lightning (represented by the letter Z) was equivalent to Thor's hammer (represented by the letter T). Another interesting facet of this particular line of reasoning is that Thor's hammer was often referred to as "**The Hammer Of The Gods**". Both Page and Plant often used the phrase "The Hammer Of The Gods" when referring to Zeppelin's sound. Small representations of Thor's Hammer were used by the people of ancient Scandinavia to ward off evil. Examples of these amulets are on display in museums throughout Scandinavia and many include decorations similar to the coptic or goetic style of Page's symbol.

Another inconclusive link is drawn through various occult societies of the 19th century. The one that claims the oldest lineage is the **Rosicrucian Order** (one branch of which is known as AMORC). They profess to be able to trace their history back about 3500 years to ancient Egypt. In the mid 1800's the Rosicrucian's enjoyed something of a renaissance in Europe that led to the flowering of many (somewhat more exotic) societies. Whereas the Rosicrucians claimed to be a purely unbigoted, unbiased brotherhood, whose aims are seemingly the pursuit of honest intellectual ideals (they have no time for hocus-pocus, witchcraft or any of the other things traditionally associated with the occult), the various splinter groups were apparently manned by some extremely convincing, but outrageously imaginative people. One of these, a certain **Madame Helene Blavatsky**, founded **The Theosophical Society** and as its head she wrote many bizarre and wonderful tales of mystery and imagination.

Fig. 6

Another splinter group of the Rosicrucians was **The Hermetic Order Of The Golden Dawn**, whose equally improbable charter leads a path right to the door of **Aleister Crowley**. (For those who don't already know, Page bought Crowley's old house in Scotland.) The connections become even more intriguing when you find Jones symbol (Fig. 6) on the spine of a book by AP Sinnett written in 1886 called "**Incidents In The Life Of Madame Blavatsky**" (Fig. 7). One of Blavatsky's own books "**The Secret Doctrine**" also included an elaborate description of the lost continent of **Lemuria**.

The concept of the legendary lost continent can be traced back to the Greek Philosopher **Plato**, who in his book "**Timaeus & Critias**" outlined the first evidence of the Atlantis myth. However, he also stated that the story came from **Solon** (another Greek born some time earlier) and it turns out Solon is generally accepted as one of the earliest Rosicrucians. This belief in the missing continent pro-

Fig. 7

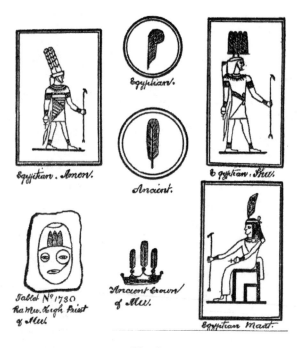

Fig. 8

duced some startling theories in the 19th century, and various manifestations of **Atlantis, Lemuria, Pan,** and **Mu** became part of the mythology of the Rosicrucians, the Theosophists and many other mystical orders.

One of the latter proponents of these theories was **James Churchward** whose books of the 1920's and 1930's brought him to prominence with their fantastic tales of the missing continent that he called *Mu*. (In fact he stole the name from two French eccentrics.) Churchward was born in the 1850's and no doubt was listening closely as the debate raged around him. Later, he expressed the opinion that Mu was the mother-land of all mankind and that Darwin was totally wrong about evolution.

In his book "**The Sacred Symbols Of Mu**" (Fig.8) Churchward revealed himself to be a man with an interest in history, combined with a wild imagination. While most academics would sug-gest there is no concrete evidence to support the lost continent theory, (other than recent evidence at Akritiri) Churchward would have you believe he knew what colors of clothes the inhabitants wore. Churchward, like Blavatsky and many others before him, had an audience who could be easily duped by a little fact blended with a lot of fiction. Certainly his brief colorful comments about the sacred background of the feather symbol are lib-erally peppered with facts, but there can be little doubt that his book's representation of the feather is the source for Plant's symbol (Fig. 9).

Fig. 9

Robert Plant: *"We'd decided that the album shouldn't be called Led Zeppelin IV and we were wondering what it should be. Then each of us decided to go away and choose a metaphorical-type symbol which somehow would represent each one of us individually - be it a* *state of mind, an opinion or something we felt strongly about or whatever. My symbol was drawn from sacred symbols of the ancient Mu civilisation which existed about 15,000 years ago as part of a lost continent somewhere in the Pacific Ocean between China and Mexico. All sorts of things can be tied in with Mu civilisation even the Easter Island effigies. These Mu people left stone tablets with their symbols inscribed into them all over the place . . . in Mexico, Egypt, Ethiopia, India, China and other places, and they all date from the same time period. The Chinese say these people came from the East and the Mexicans say they came from the West . . . obviously it was somewhere in between. My personal symbol does have a further meaning, and all I can suggest is that people look it up in a suitable reference work."*

Churchward: *"The feather is another of the very prominent Ancient Sacred Symbols; it symbolized Truth."*

Plant: *"The feather, a symbol on which all sorts of philosophies have been based, and which has a very interesting heritage. For instance, it represents courage to many red Indian tribes...... I like people to lay down the truth. No bullshit. That's what the feather in the circle is all about."*

This takes us back to the Rosicrucians who (perhaps not) coincidentally hold Truth above all else and the pursuit of Truth in its absolute form is part of their charter (at least that is the implication of **Spencer Lewis** a prominent Rosicrucian of the early 20th century). On one final note Rosicrucian meetings are held on ....**Thursday**.

In some early interviews the band alluded to Icelandic runes, although Page later commented *".. the symbols were not Icelandic. That was just a red herring-type rumour. Only the middle two are actually runes. What happened was that we all chose a symbol and the four together became the title of the album."*

Runes were an archaic form of writing that were used by various different cultures, amongst them the ancient Scandinavians. Runes were all but wiped from the face of the earth as a form of communication by the early Christians, but many had survived since before the time of Christ. One of the most ancient is the **gammadion** (Fig. 10).

The gammadion was one of the most revered of ancient religious symbols. In Sanskrit it means "fortunate" it was holy to cultures in Troy, Greece, Egypt, China, South America, North America (the Navaho), India, Persia, and Scandinavia, and most significantly one form of it

Fig. 10

represented *Thor's hammer* (fig. 11). In the late 1800's and early part of this century, it was a symbol of Hermetic magic that came to be adopted by various mystical societies, including **The Hermetic Order Of The Golden Dawn**. Aleister Crowley wrote a pam-

Fig. 11

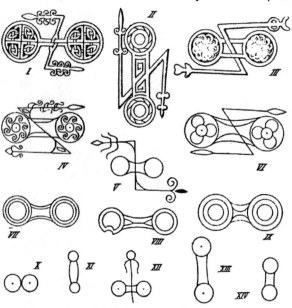

SCOTTISH GAMMADION AND RING SYMBOLS

From sculptured stones : I, St. Vigeans ; II, Monifieth ; III, Elgin ; IV, Dunnichen ; VI, Bourtie ; VII, Abbotsford ; VIII, Newton ; IX, Golspie ; X, Stonehaven. From caves at East Wemyss, Fife : V, XI, XII, XIII, XIV. After Stuart's *Sculptured Stones*.

Fig. 12

phlet about the gammadion in 1910. Spencer Lewis also outlined the evolution of the cross, showing a clear link between the gammadion and the Rosicrucians. There are many examples of the gammadion that are very similar in nature to elements of Page's symbol, almost all of which appear in Scotland. (Fig. 12). Agrippa also used a basic gammadion as one of the symbols for **Saturn** *and combined it with symbols for Jupiter and Mars* (Thor's analog in the Roman pantheon). (Fig. 12a) Although Page's symbol is clearly not a gammadion in its traditional appearance, the connections drawn between "The Hammer of the Gods", Lead, Saturn, Crowley (and his home in Scotland), Thursday and the Rosicrucians, creates an intriguing combination that seems to stretch the bounds of coincidence.

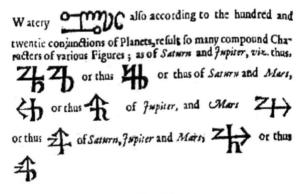

Fig. 12a

Robert Plant: *"You may not believe this, but Pagey once took me aside and said 'Look, I'm* *going to tell you the meaning of this once, and then I shan't ever mention it again—or at least, not for a long, long time anyway', and would you believe that I have since forgotten what it was and now Pagey won't tell me. If I know Pagey it'll turn up in some long lost book. That's the only light I can throw on it."* **(See bibliography.)**

John Bonham: *"The runes are symbols that simply apply to each of us. I wouldn't like to state what they mean. Each one of us picked one."*

On the subject of Bonham's symbol **Robert Plant** commented, *"I suppose it's the trilogy, man, woman and child. I suspect it has something to do with the mainstay of all people's beliefs. At one point, though, in Pittsburgh I think, we observed that it was also the emblem of Ballantine beer."*

The symbol for Ballantine's beer is actually an inverted version, with two rings at the top and one below, however the German Krupp corporation, ironically a manufacturer of heavy artillery, has been using the sym-

Fig. 13

bol in Bonham's exact configuration for decades. Bonham actually extracted his symbol (Fig. 13) from a book by the celebrated typographer **Rudolf Koch** called "**The Book Of Signs**". (Fig. 14.)

This is another early sign for the Trinity.

Each circle has its own centre and is therefore complete in itself; at the same time it has a large section in common with each of the other circles, though only the small central shield is covered by all three circles. In this shield they possess a new central point, the real heart of the whole figure.

Fig. 14

At this point it becomes increasingly clear that most symbology has a different meaning to each person. Although the symbol may have a traditional meaning it can be reinterpreted by any individual to mean what they want it to mean. This makes the definition of the symbol almost impossible without the context, and, without the cooperation of the individual, the context is indecipherable.

Jimmy Page: *"John Paul Jones' symbol, the second from the left, was found in a book about runes and was said to represent a person who is both confident and competent, because it was difficult to draw accurately. Bonzo's came from the same book—he just picked it out* *because he liked it."* The Koch explanation for Jones symbol makes reference to another symbol, both of which carry the same meaning. (Fig. 15.)

The only definite conclusion that one can draw from the title of Led Zeppelin's fourth album is that symbols, runes and talismans inevitably mean different things to different people. The interpretations are so variegated that without the band revealing their original intent in detail we are not likely to ever know the translation. Those who

𝔗𝔴𝔬 𝔰𝔦𝔤𝔫𝔰 𝔲𝔰𝔢𝔡 𝔱𝔬 𝔢𝔵𝔬𝔯𝔠𝔦𝔰𝔢 𝔢𝔳𝔦𝔩 𝔰𝔭𝔦𝔯𝔦𝔱𝔰. 𝔍𝔫 𝔱𝔥𝔢 𝔠𝔞𝔰𝔢 𝔬𝔣 𝔟𝔬𝔱𝔥 𝔱𝔥𝔢𝔰𝔢 𝔰𝔦𝔤𝔫𝔰, 𝔞𝔰 𝔴𝔦𝔱𝔥 𝔱𝔥𝔢 𝔭𝔢𝔫𝔱𝔞𝔤𝔯𝔞𝔪 𝔞𝔫𝔡 𝔱𝔥𝔢 𝔬𝔠𝔱𝔬𝔤𝔯𝔞𝔪, 𝔦𝔱 𝔦𝔰 𝔴𝔬𝔯𝔱𝔥𝔶 𝔬𝔣 𝔫𝔬𝔱𝔢 𝔱𝔥𝔞𝔱 𝔱𝔥𝔢𝔶 𝔠𝔞𝔩𝔩 𝔣𝔬𝔯 𝔞 𝔠𝔢𝔯𝔱𝔞𝔦𝔫 𝔡𝔢𝔵𝔱𝔢𝔯𝔦𝔱𝔶, 𝔞𝔫𝔡 𝔱𝔥𝔞𝔱 𝔞 𝔠𝔩𝔲𝔪𝔰𝔶 𝔭𝔢𝔯𝔰𝔬𝔫 𝔴𝔬𝔲𝔩𝔡 𝔟𝔢 𝔲𝔫𝔞𝔟𝔩𝔢 𝔱𝔬 𝔡𝔯𝔞𝔴 𝔱𝔥𝔢𝔪.

Fig. 15

are interested in seeking further meaning may perhaps find it interesting to purchase a copy of Nintendo's early Star Trek video game cartridge. Captain Kirk and Mr Spock are required to fathom the mysteries of ꝥ ⚠⊛ⓘ to progress their way through the maze, alternatively you might want to check the bibliography at the end of this book!

THE COVER AND VARIATIONS

Beyond the obvious mystery of the four symbols another interesting and often discussed aspect of Led Zeppelin's fourth album are the cover graphics. (Fig. 15a)

Page explained how the artwork developed with no title or printing on the cover. *" It came to the point where we thought, Right, on the next album we'll make it an untitled album with no information on it whatsoever, virtually saying if you don't like it, you don't have to buy it for the name.*

"The words 'Led Zeppelin' do not occur anywhere on the cover, and all the other usual credits are missing too. I had to talk like hell to get that done . . . the record company told us we were committing profes-sional suicide.

"I remember being in an Atlantic office for two hours with a lawyer who was saying, 'You've gotta have this' so I said, 'Alright. Run it on the inside bag. Print your Rockefeller plaza or what-

Fig. 15a

Black Dog (4.55)
(Page, Plant, Jones)
Rock And Roll (3.40)
(Page, Plant, Jones, Bonham)
The Battle Of Evermore (5.38)
(Page, Plant)
Stairway To Heaven (7.55)
(Page, Plant)
Misty Mountain Hop (4.39)
(Page, Plant, Jones)
Four Sticks (4.49)
(Page, Plant)
Going To California (3.31)
(Page, Plant)
When The Levee Breaks (7.08)
(Page, Plant, Jones, Bonham, Memphis Minnie)

ever it is down there.' Of course they didn't want to have a rerun on it so there it is. It was a hard job but fortunately we were in a position to say, "This is what we want" because we had attained the status whereby that album was going to sell a lot of albums. We didn't think it was going to sell as many as it did, but we thought it was going to sell a lot because of the whole vibe of the band and everything else. We said we just wanted to rely purely on the music."

The band's manager **Peter Grant** later declared that the idea of no title at all was his: *"I'm the one who said forget the title. Let's not have any title at all. All we had on it were those symbols, that's all."*

What began as an attempt to shrug off the "hype" accusations that were still dogging the band, ended up as one of the great accidental marketing moves of all time. By leaving the album jacket untarnished by titles or logos, the artwork itself became the focal point for discussion amongst the fans and critics; the implication being that there must be some heavy mystical significance to the pictures. Even as recently as the 1990's authors have speculated about who the mysterious figure on the cover might be. One notable theory identifies him as one **George Pickingill,** a high profile occultist from late 19th century England. Apparently the likeness between the two is uncanny and rumour has it that one of Pickingill's students also taught Aleister Crowley. Another story suggests that there were several outtakes of the "Old Man" photo session sitting around in Swansong's filing cabinet years later, thus undermining the Pickingill connection, although these may have been outtakes of the session of *the picture on the wall amongst the slums.* Page however stated: *"I remember he (Plant) bought the picture in a junk shop in Reading, I was with him at the time."*

Shortly after the record's release Page attempted to clarify the significance of the art-work: *"The old man on the cover, carrying the wood, is in harmony with nature. He takes from nature and gives back to the land. It's a natural circle. It's right. His old cottage gets pulled down and they put him in these urban slums - old slums, terrible places. The old man is also the Hermit of the Tarot cards - a symbol of self-reliance and mystical wisdom. Some people say it has allusions of Jolman Hunt but it hasn't. It actu-*

ally comes from the idea from the tarot card, the hermit and so the ascension to the beacon and the light of truth. The hermit is holding out the light of truth and enlightenment to a young man at the foot of the hill. If you know the tarot cards, you'll know what the hermit means. The inside was painted by a friend of mine, Barrington Colby. Unfortunately the negatives were a bit duff so you can't quite read an Oxfam poster on the side of a building on the back of the jacket. It's the poster where someone is lying dead on a stretcher and it says that everyday someone receives relief from hunger. You can just make it out on the jacket if you've seen the poster before. But other than that, there's no writing on the jacket at all.

"The whole LP was an experiment really because everything was underplayed, rightly or wrongly. When you haven't put out an album for a year and there's this huge enigma that's blown up, and then you put out an album with no title whatsoever . . . and with no reference to the group whatsoever apart from the piece of plastic inside, then some people would consider that to be suicide. But the whole thing had to be done to satisfy our own minds after all the crap that had gone down in the newspaper".

John Bonham's interpretation of the front cover is a little different: *"The new LP. The cover means whatever people want to read into it. For me it means: I'd rather live in an old house than a block of flats."*

Robert Plant: *"With every cover we've had before, what we've asked for hasn't been what we've got. We wanted a cover with no writing on it, not the Atlantic symbol or the 'uptight and outa sight' bit."* The latter remark is in reference to an Atlantic fan club address that appeared on many releases at that time.

One interesting aspect of the artwork mystery is that in many foreign territories where the album was released, the band apparently relinquished their normal iron-clad grip over quality and content. The end result is a bizarre series of half-hearted reproductions of the cover art. In Greece for example it looks as if a copy of the jacket was pinned to a wall with thumb tacks and then photographed complete with pin holes and coffee stains. In South America the symbols appeared on the front cover and sometimes so did the words **"The New Led Zeppelin Album"** (Fig. 15b). In Russia the "Old Man" picture on the front was entirely replaced with a different picture in the frame! (Fig. 15c)

The final corruption of what was surely one of the most intriguing record sleeves of all time came in the 1980's when Atlantic

Fig. 15b

Fig. 15c

finally released the first CD version. As the band had split up four years earlier there was now no one left to "defend the faith" and so all of the uniquely mysterious elements of the cover were suddenly blown into oblivion and replaced with the inevitable logo's and copyright bull.

Fig. 15d

In the 1980's some other curiosities appeared. The record was re-released on pink vinyl in the UK and there are some rumours of a white vinyl pressing in the USA. There was also an extremely rare gold vinyl version from Canada. In 1989 HMV record chain in the UK acquired permission to release the vinyl album and the CD in limited edition box sets. The box showed a miniature version of the cover and each one was numbered out of 3,500 copies. (Fig. 15d) Inside the box was an album sized booklet with notes by noted Zep biographer and journalist **Chris Welch**.

In many of the smaller music markets (such as Venezuela, Peru and Israel) it was packaged in a single pocket cover with no gatefold. In Thailand, Taiwan, Korea and probably many other markets it was pirated with an assortment of inferior cover designs. (Figs. 15e,f,g,h)

Fig. 15e   Fig. 15f

Fig. 15g   Fig. 15h

Fig. 15i

Besides the inevitable cassette releases, it was also released on pre-recorded quarter inch four track reel-to-reel tape in the USA by **Stereotape**. There was also a version on the dreaded 8-Track format, which saw the song order shifted around to be Black Dog, Four Sticks, Going To California, Stairway To Heaven, Misty Mountain Hop, The Battle Of Evermore, Rock And Roll, When The Levee Breaks (at least it was complete which can't

Fig. 15j

be said for the 8 track of the first album which saw the middle of one track edited out!)

In 1990 the first official Led Zeppelin "Greatest Hits" package was released with a four CD or six LP box set (Fig 15i). It included seven of the eight tracks from the fourth album and also featured some innovative new artwork of the four symbols (one on each CD). The only track which didn't make it onto the four disc set was Four Sticks which was held back until the second box set in 1992. (Fig. 15j) Another two CD set was released in the UK and Japan which featured five tracks from the fourth album. (Fig. 15k) This "Remasters"

Fig. 15k

package was also available through Time-Life on American TV and then ultimately in a booklet format in the stores. (Fig. 15l) In 1999 five tracks were featured in the greatest hits package "Early Days" (Fig. 15m) (which was subsequently re-released as a double CD with "Latter Days" in 2002).

Fig. 15l

Fig. 15m

Four tracks also appeared on the "Mothership" hits package in 2007, along with live versions on the DVD bonus package.

SINGLES

The only official singles to be released from 𝄢 ⚖ ⊕ ① were **Black Dog**, backed with **Misty Mountain Hop** (Atlantic 2849) and **Rock And Roll** backed with **Four Sticks** (Atlantic 2865). The former reached the #15 position in the American charts while the latter peaked at #47. Neither single was released with a picture sleeve in the USA but there are multiple different sleeves from other countries.

Black Dog / Misty Mountain Hop
U.S. Atlantic 2849
U.S. Atlantic OS 13129
Argentina Atlantic 2091175
Australia Atlantic 45-2849
Canada Atlantic AT 2849
Canada Atlantic GS 45848
France Atlantic 10103
Germany Atlantic 10-103
Greece Atlantic 2091 175
Holland Atlantic 2091 175
Italy Atlantic K 10103
Japan Atlantic P-136A
Mexico Atlantic 2207 024
Mexico Atlantic G1125
New Zealand Atlantic 88
Portugal Atlantic N 28-118
Portugal Atlantic 10103
Spain Hispavox HS 775
South Africa Atlantic ATS 568
Sweden Atlantic 10103

In the smaller territories there are various other singles and EPs that almost certainly didn't get the band's approval. In South Africa Rock And Roll was backed with Going To California (Atlantic 590). In Venezuela the two A-sides were back to

Black Dog/ Misty Mountain Hop Singles

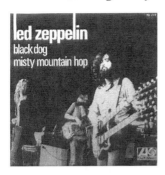

France

Germany

Holland

Italy

Japan

Mexico

Rock and Roll/ Four Sticks Singles

France

Germany

Holland

Spain

Japan

Portugal

Rock And Roll / Four Sticks

U.S. Atlantic 2865
U.S. Atlantic OS 13130
Australia Atlantic 45-2865
Brazil Atco ATCS 10.005
Canada Atlantic AT 2865
Canada Atlantic GS 45849
France Atlantic 10156
Germany Atlantic 10156
Greece Atlantic 2091 190
Holland Atlantic 2091 190
Japan Atlantic P-105A
Portugal Atlantic N 28-128
Spain Hispavox HS 823

back Black Dog/ Rock And Roll (Atlantic 5-011). In Taiwan there were at least a half dozen different EPs that combined various fourth album tracks with other Zep material and sometimes other artists. One example is a Taiwanese EP of Black Dog, Rock and Roll, Misty Mountain Hop and Going to California. (Fig. 15n)

These were all certainly released without Atlantic or the band's

Fig. 15n

permission and included When The Levee Breaks and several different pirate pressings of Stairway To Heaven. (Fig. 15o-p)

One interesting novelty is an Atlantic EP

Fig. 15o

Fig. 15p

Fig. 16

from Australia called **Acoustically Led Zeppelin** (Atlantic EPA 228 - Fig. 16). This official release has the distinction of being the only official commercial 7" release to include Stairway To Heaven and one can only wonder how it slipped through Peter Grant's net.

The final gem in the history of this album's rarities is from Canada. In the mid 1980's Atlantic announced that the album would be going Diamond (sales of one million units). To promote this auspicious event, which had only been achieved by a half a dozen albums previously, a promotion was launched whereby the one millionth copy would be re-mastered and inscribed with a secret message. The lucky person would be able to claim a diamond and gold Zeppelin brooch/pin. The prize was quite desirable as the diamond was supposedly one carat, and so hoards of retailers and punters flocked to the shops and snapped up the latest pressing run. After many months no one had claimed the prize and it was duly forgotten, until finally after two years a young lady from Ontario came forward. It seems she had bought the album years before, but had never listened to side two as she had bought it exclusively for Stairway To Heaven. The audio message was inscribed on side two between Four Sticks and Going To California.

PROMOS

In early 1972 Atlantic records applied enormous pressure on the group to encourage the release of **Stairway To Heaven** as a single. The band had performed a successful tour of the UK in March of 1971 and had followed up with sell-out tours of the USA and Japan in August and September. The highlight of the new show was the latest in a string of anthems for the band, a song that demanded radio airplay.

Fig. 17

Atlantic Records had been receiving a constant stream of requests from programmers around the world asking for a single, but the band and Peter Grant were adamant that the

Fig. 17a

song should not be taken out of context from the rest of the record. Finally, it was determined that a 7" promotional-only single would be released and sent out to radio. This particular single came in a blue, black and white deluxe sleeve (Fig. 17) and is now much sought after by collectors around the world. (Fig. 17a)

Fig. 17b

There were also various pirate releases of Stairway within the USA. One of these came as a picture disc and was backed with "Hey Hey What Can I Do" which had only been previously available as a B-side to "The Immigrant Song". (Fig. 17b)

In 1991 Atlantic released an unprecedented promo package that was to celebrate the twentieth anniversary of the song. Although it was only supposed to be for promotional use, many copies made their way onto the collector's market. This package was an 11" by 7" colour gatefold

Fig. 18

sleeve (Fig. 18) that included both a seven inch vinyl single and a CD single of Stairway. When the sleeve was opened it revealed a pop-up display of the old man with the sticks on his back carrying a Zeppelin. A lyric sheet was also enclosed as well as an explanation about the song's history. It was without a doubt the nicest promo item ever done for a Zeppelin release and yet the song still wasn't released as a single.

THE RECORDING

Early song construction for 🎵 🎵 🎵 ① began at one of Robert Plant's favourite retreats in North Wales in May 1970, a small cottage near **Bron-y-Aur** (which means Golden Breast).

Armed with several guitars, a couple of helpers, a tape recorder, and a dog, Plant and Page sequestered themselves and composed a batch of songs that were destined to be spread across five albums. The bulk of these songs would appear on the third album in October of 1970 but several would make it through to the fourth, fifth, sixth and the posthumous release **Coda**.

What was clearly an inspirational setting for them, Bron-y-Aur gave birth to a sound that had not previously been associated with Led Zeppelin. Plant and Page in the isolation of the Welsh mountains (where supposedly they were without electrical power) could only use acousti-cal instruments and so many of the songs com-posed there were created with simple guitar structures and basic percussion. Some of the songs that came from this session were *Bron-y-Aur Stomp, Bron-y-Aur, That's The Way, Hey Hey What Can I Do, Down By The Seaside, Poor Tom, and Gallow's Pole*. This softer sound followed through into continuing rehearsals at Headley Grange (Fig. 19) and although the bootleg

Fig. 19

sources are not identified too clearly, it is possible that *No Quarter, Going To California, The Rover,* and possibly *Stairway To Heaven* may all have begun life at Bron-y-Aur.

Page had been demoing some of the early ideas at home: *"I had a unit called the New Vista. It was the deck that was used to record Live At Leeds. I thought it was a fabulous unit, really. When they were trying to get away from valves, one of the things they developed was the Vista and the Transistor. The Vista did sound very valvey. I used to do a lot of overlays and such...I had the eight-track at home."*

These early demos of Stairway can be heard on many different bootlegs including the two CD's **Stairway Sessions** (Fig. 20) and **Ultra**

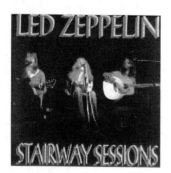

Fig. 20

Rare Tracks. In a later interview Page revealed that he put together reasonable demos for the rest of the band to hear, some of which included overdubs.

In December 1970 the band moved into Island Studios in Chiswick, a suburb of West London, and began laying down basic tracks for the album. **Page:** "*We started off doing some tracks at the new Island Studios in London in December '70, but after that we went to our house, Headley Grange in Hampshire, a place where we frequently rehearse.*"

As on previous occasions the band chose to use eminent engineer **Andrew Johns** to assist with the recording. Andrew's brother Glyn had worked on the first Led Zeppelin album and both brothers had a reputation for being two of the best engineers in the business. Andy had worked with **The Rolling Stones,** and one of his sidelines was running the Stone's Mobile recording studio which was one of the first of its kind in England. **Ian Stewart**, who had played piano with the Stones in their early days, was responsible for the managing of the studio. Stewart and Page had worked together before when Stewart had played piano on the **Yardbird's** "Little Games" album.

Andy Johns: *"I had just done Sticky Fingers with the Stones, and we used their mobile truck on that. So I believe I suggested using the truck to Jimmy. We used Mick's house in Stargroves for a bit, but Jimmy didn't want to stay there because Mick wanted too much money."*

Headley Grange

Built in 1795. Two storeys. Stone structure with a tiled roof. Sash windows. Five pedimented dormers with decorative fascia boards. A long low wing and other adjoining additions. It was converted into a private dwelling in 1870.

Originally Headley Workhouse, in the 1970's the building was rented out for six or seven years to various bands (including Genesis). Led Zeppelin used the house on at least three separate occasions. Various songs for Led Zeppelin III, Physical Graffiti and ⚡ 🪶 ⭕ Ⓘ were written and recorded there.

Photos Courtesy John Smith & Winchester Reference Library

The most famous stairway in rock and roll history pictured in 1996. "The Minstrel Gallery", as it is known by the family who have owned Headley Grange for four generations, was chosen by Led Zeppelin because of its extraordinary acoustics. While the rest of the band performed in the drawing room, which was converted into a makeshift studio with empty egg cartons stuck to the walls as acoustic baffles, John Bonham's drumkit was set up at the foot of the stairs. Microphones were draped from the railings on the floors above to capture the unique ambiance.

The often sampled drum intro from "When the Levee Breaks" and many other significant moments in Led Zeppelin's repertoire were created here. The photographer commented, "The stairway is quite extraordinary. It seems to go on upwards forever."

Picture
Courtesy
Jo Broom,

P. & D.
Markham

Johns' reference to Stargroves is not reflected in any of the documentation about the album. The band certainly used Stargroves for the recording of their fifth album and at least one track on Physical Graffiti. After leaving Stargroves the band moved back into an old haunt that had provided them with the ambiance they needed when they had recorded the third album.

Andy Johns: *"Jimmy found this old, beat-up farmhouse called Headley Grange, so we brought the truck up there. I think we had three or four stories in which to run around in. It was a lot of fun. Using the mobile truck allows you to have a control room on wheels. It's a bit narrow, like a corridor, so your ability to monitor a situation isn't as good as in a proper studio. You end up talking to the band through a closed-circuit camera and a microphone instead of through the studio glass. It can get a bit impersonal, but the advantage is that the band is more at home. At a place like the farmhouse in Headley Grange, you had a fire-place, people bringing you cups of tea. It's much nicer than a studio."*

Page: *"Apparently, it was a Victorian work house at one time, that's what I was told. It was a sort of three storey house with a huge open hall with a staircase going up... I loved it. It was a pret-ty austere place, I loved the atmosphere of it. I really did personally. The others got a bit spooked out by it. For some reason, we decided to take the Stones mobile truck there . . . because we were* *used to the place. It was familiar territory. We had even lived there during long rehearsal sessions. It seemed ideal - as soon as we thought of an idea, we put it down on tape. In a way, it was a good method. The only thing wrong was that we'd get so excited about an idea that we'd really rush to finish its format to get it on tape. It was like a quick productivity thing. It was just so exciting to have all the facilities there."*

Plant: *"Most of the mood for this new album was brought about in settings that we hadn't come across before. We were living in this old falling-apart mansion way out in the country. The mood was incredible. We could put something down on the spot and hear the results immediately. There was no waiting around until you could get into the studio. It doesn't relate to anything we've done before - it was that much longer after the third album, so it's that much different."*

Headley Grange was originally built in 1795 as a "Poor House". It was the centre of a well-publicized riot in 1830 and was converted into a private home in 1870. It is located in the village of Headley in eastern Hampshire (a county in southern England on the border of Page's home county of Surrey) and even today the building is "listed" as a landmark due to its colorful history. A local author, **John Owen Smith**, wrote a book about the building called "One Monday In November - The Story Of The Selborne and Headley Workhouse Riots of 1830".

John Owen Smith: *"Some of my friends well remember listening to the "noise" from the Grange - at one point one of their mothers went over to complain that her children were trying to revise for an exam, and the music stopped - "they were quite nice about it," my friend said. Others remember listening to the music, with varying degrees of approval, as they worked their allotments just across the road. The Grange is not the only place in Headley with a 'pop' history.* **Fleetwood Mac** *lived in another big house in the village for a while."*

Recording continued at Headley Grange through the month of January 1971 and possibly into February. On February 9th Page and Andy Johns arrived in Los Angeles to begin a ten day mixing session at **Sunset Sound Studios**. Sunset had a remarkable musical background. It had been used by an incredible range of major talents over the years, including The Doors, Bing Crosby, John Lennon, The Who, The Stones, and many other world class producers and artists.

Plant: *"Jimmy took all the material over to Sunset Sound in Los Angeles with a very famous producer who said it was THE studio, and did the mixes. We finished recording in February and the idea was to mix it there and get it out in March. But he brought the tapes back and they sounded terrible, so we had to start mixing all over again. We were disgusted at the amount of time it had taken to get the album finished. The sound of the* mixing room that Andy Johns took Jimmy to was really duff . . .The whole story of the fourth album reads like a nightmare. The sound had to be remixed again in this country, then a master tape of one track 'Four Sticks' was lost."

Page: "That's when the fiasco started, because I was pretty confident that it sounded alright to me. In that room it had sounded great anyway. The trouble was that the speakers were lying. It wasn't the balance, it was the actual sound that was on the tape. When we played it back in England, it sounded like it had gone through this odd process."

Andy Johns: "I wanted to mix in LA cos I was seeing this chick and I'd mixed an album there with Sky (who became The Knack) and so when we got to Sunset they'd changed the monitors, so we decided to use another room. That was a mistake we should have just gone home, but I didn't want to and I don't think Jimmy did either we were having a good time you know? Anyway we only worked for about 10 days by the time we left. When we got back the other guys in the band wanted to hear what we'd done and so we went into Olympic Studio One to do the playbacks, which was another mistake. The only thing that sounds good in that room is stuff that was done there. Anyway the stuff sounded absolutely ghastly. It was a very hard 40 minutes and Jimmy and I were crouched in the corner really embarrassed. You've got to remember that mixing was *still a bit of a mystery to us, we were really young. We never took tapes home to listen or we might have known. We would have checked them today. I know that one of the tracks done there we ended up using, I think it was Levee. I've since done other things there. The Stones "Exile On Main Street" was done there and my brother did some stuff there that sounded as good as anything I've heard. Anyway we went back to Island and it took a bit longer. After that I guess they didn't need old Andy, you know who needs that? I think the album ended up sounding OK. "*

After realising that the Sunset mix was not going to stand up, Page and Johns returned to Island in London to remix seven of the eight tracks. The only track that was retained with the Sunset mix was *"When The Levee Breaks".* There were several other songs that were recorded which were left over until Physical Graffiti. *"Down By The Seaside", "Boogie With Stu"* and a couple of songs from the third album sessions at Island. These were listed in the 1990's Remasters series as being recorded in 1974.

Andy Johns: "*Those were left over from 1970. No way those are from 1974.*"

Even with the problems surrounding the album, Plant returned to Sunset Sound to work on some of his solo albums in the eighties and nineties.

In early July the final tapes were delivered to **Trident Studios** in London for mastering. The first cuts for the USA (ST-A-712285/A-13749 and ST-A-712286/A-13750) were delivered to the pressing plant, **Presswell Records**, on July 19th 1971. Two more sets of lacquers were also ordered for Monarch Pressing Plant and Philips Pressing Plant the same day. A second set of masters was created at **Apple Studios** in London (ST-712285-B and ST-712286-B) and also delivered to Presswell. On August 20th four more sets of mothers were created from recut masters (ST-A-712285 C,D,E,F and ST-A-712286 C,D,E,F) and were distributed to Presswell, Monarch and Philips.

		REQUEST FOR MASTERS							
REQUESTED BY: Manfred Bormann			45 ☐	LP ☒	Other: ☐				
DESIGNATED BY:							DATE July 19, 1971		
MASTERED BY:									
MASTER NO.	ARTIST	TITLE	TIME	DATE MASTERED	DATE SENT TO PLANT	PLATING PLANT	PRESSING PLANT	QUANT. OF PARTS	CAT. NO.
ST-A-712285	LED ZEPPELIN	SIDE ONE					PRESSWELL	set	ATLANTIC
22398		1. BLACK DOG	4:55				MONARCH	of lacquers	SD 7208
22399		2. ROCK AND ROLL	3:40				PHILIPS		
22400		3. BATTLE OF EVERMORE	5:38						
22401		4. STAIRWAY TO HEAVEN	7:55						
		TOTAL:	22:08						
ST-A-712286	LED ZEPPELIN	SIDE TWO				"	"	"	"
22402		1. MISTY MOUNTAIN HOP	4:99						
22403		2. FOUR STICKS	4:49						
22404		3. GOING TO CALIFORNIA	3:36						
22405		4. WHEN THE LEVEE BREAKS	7:08						
		TOTAL:	23:12						
REASON IF REMASTERING:									
MASTERING INSTRUCTIONS IF ANY:									

The Masters request sheet for ⚡ △ ❀ ◯

THE PRESS

Up until 1971, although the music journals had been reasonably generous, the mainstream press had been fairly condescending and sometimes even dismissive of Led Zeppelin. When the band released their fourth album it became virtually impossible for the press to ignore them. Sellout tours of Europe, the UK, the USA and Japan had cemented the band's position in the vanguard of popular music. Their previous albums had defied prediction, both musically and commercially, and their popularity with the fans was undeniable. A hugely successful radio broadcast by the BBC in April 1971, during which the band previewed the new record, and a highly visible **Back to the Clubs** tour were all shrewd decisions taken by the band and Peter Grant to make points with the only people that mattered to them, the fans. **Melody Maker** and **New Musical Express** had a couple of staff writers who genuinely liked the band. These advocates were given plenty of encouragement by the band and were invited into the inner circle.

One of these writers, **Chris Welch**, was to become a name that the British fans would associate with Led Zeppelin. His enthusiastic interviews and columns in Melody Maker were one of the few high points for the band's fans in the British media. Whenever there was an article by Welch about Zep you knew it would be informative and positive. Another journalist, **Ritchie Yorke**, who worked as a foreign correspondent for the British music weeklies from his office at the **Globe and Mail** in Toronto Canada, also became a favourite, and his positive reports from the USA and Canada were a welcome change from some of the ill-informed press that was pumped out by the forest-load in the USA. In later years both Welch and Yorke would write books about their association with Led Zeppelin that were filled with anecdotes and insights into some memorable moments. Chris Welch was in attendance at the band's concert in Belfast Ireland on March 5th 1971. In his review of the show afterwards he mentioned the first public performance of a song from the album—Stairway To Heaven.

Welch: *"An excellent ballad which displayed Robert's developing lyricism."* In later years Welch himself would relate his own amazement at the song's enormous growth in popularity. He also wrote the liner notes for the HMV box set release in 1985 in which he re-iterated many of his earlier impressions, but also included two reviews typical of the time, one positive, one negative.

Disc & Music Echo: *"If Zep III gave the first indications that their music was by no means confined to power rock then this new album consolidates their expanding maturity. The eight cuts contained herein follow through with unbridled confidence expounding in greater detail the ideas* *formulated on the previous collection."*

Sounds: *"A much overrated album...the first track Black Dog clatters along with all the grace and finesse of a farmyard chicken. Stairway To Heaven...palls dramatically with repeated plays inducing first boredom and then catatonia."* The latter review might offer a partial explanation why *Sounds* went out of business, this having been written much later, just prior to the paper's demise. However, it suffices to illustrate the totally disparate views that the band had to face when it came to dealing with the press.

Page: *"I know that there were originally quite a few people who picked up on the fourth album and gave it a good write up, but there were the usuals who gave it a good slamming. In England was where we got a major slamming. But 'Stairway To Heaven' was just there. Up to that point we'd been aware of all the crap that had gone on more than anybody, obviously because we were right on the end of it, and we knew there was this huge enigma that had blown up. As far as we were concerned, whatever we did we always delivered the best we possibly could. From the first sort of blues-oriented album, the second one was rock & roll, I think they assumed the third was going to be, you know, yet again rocking on, and the added fact that Zep 2 was like "THE" classic rock album and I think they expected... like... I know the record company expected a follow-up to "Whole Lotta Love" which obviously* wasn't on this. But... However, we always stick to how we were shaping up at the time.

"Anyway, we never really made a point of trying to emulate something that we had done before. What we thought we were doing was right, and good and we felt it was quality music. You've gotta live by what you believe in, otherwise you might as well just forget it as far as I'm concerned. I'm speaking for all of us at that point or as well as I can believe everyone felt at that point.

"Certain things would frustrate me... I used to get the music papers and in the end I just stopped buying them. Not because of what they were writing about us but because I'd go and see a concert of somebody else and it'd be a great concert and I'd get the papers, they'd come in every Friday... and I'd look and see this concert reviewed and it would be like, "What the hell is this all about?" It'd have nothing to do whatever with the concert I saw. And they had this policy that you were God one minute and shit the next! To keep the controversy going and sell papers, so I thought sod this I don't need to read this I'd rather listen."

THE CONCERTS

When the fourth album finally hit the world's record stores in the fourth quarter of 1971 the band had already played over 200 concerts, many of which were double-headers. After returning from Los Angeles with the first mix of the album the band headed out onto the road with their much publicized **Back To The Clubs** tour.

Continuing with their attempts to answer their critics (who now accused the band of becoming so big that no one could get near them) Peter Grant announced that Led Zeppelin's next tour would commence in Belfast on March 5th and the band would play in many of the small venues that had booked them back in 1968. The tour would encompass thirteen shows in nearly four weeks, culminating with the **BBC In Concert** radio broadcast. As much as the fans and the clubs appreciated the gesture, the media were quick to condemn the band for leaving so many

UK
Back To The Clubs
Tour 1971
March
5th Belfast Ulster Hall
6th Dublin Boxing Stadium
9th Leeds University
10th Canterbury University
11th Southampton University
13th Bath Pavilion
14th Stoke Hanley Place
18th Newcastle Mayfair
19th Manchester University
20th Sutton Coldfield Belfry
21st Nottingham Rowing Club
23rd Marquee London
April
1st London BBC Paris Theatre

people without tickets. During the course of the tour the band continued to preview *Stairway To Heaven* and *Going To California* but it was not until they reached Scandinavia in May that the public would get a taste of the rest of the album.

Ever since their first tour together the band had used the audiences in Sweden and Denmark as a proving ground. Their first ever public performance was in Copenhagen and right through until their last major appearance in the UK at Knebworth in 1979, they would use Copenhagen as their warm up venue. On **May 3rd** the band performed at the **K.B. Hallen** in Copenhagen, a concert that is now considered a seminal moment in the band's performing career, not for its particularly exceptional performance, but because the band chose to fill the set list with a string of surprises. A fifteen song set that comprised of six of the songs from the fourth album as well as the first complete performance of *Gallow's Pole*, the first performance of *Celebration Day* (in the middle of *Communication Breakdown*!), and a twenty one minute *Whole Lotta Love* medley packed with old rock and roll standards.

Fortunately, a bootleg tape survives which chronicles this astounding show in reasonably good detail. The first and only known performance of *Four Sticks* is a tentative, but remarkable rendition, that carries hints of the version that Page and Plant recorded for their **No**

Plant & Page on stage May 3rd 1971 Copenhagen
Photographer unknown

Quarter album in 1994. *Black Dog* features some different lyrics and *Rock And Roll* is introduced as *It's Been A Long Time*. *Stairway* and *Going To California* are by now well settled into the set and immediately recognisable and *Misty Mountain Hop* is virtually demolished by the band, which may explain why it was promptly shelved for the next 18 months. The two songs omitted, *When*

The Levee Breaks and *Battle Of Evermore* would have to wait until 1975 and 1977 respectively, before they would be performed live. *Levee* made it into the set for only a handful of shows and was first performed in Rotterdam on January 11th 1975 but was dropped three shows later. *Battle* was first performed on April 1st 1977 at Dallas Memorial Auditorium and survived throughout the complete 1977 American tour.

NORTH AMERICAN TOUR 1971
AUGUST
19th Vancouver Pacific Coliseum
20th Seattle Center
21st Los Angeles Forum
22nd Los Angeles Forum
23rd Fort Worth Tarrant Convention Center
24th Dallas Memorial Auditorium
25th Houston Sam Houston Coliseum
27th San Antonio Municipal Auditorium
28th St. Louis Arena
29th New Orleans Municipal Auditorium
31st Orlando Civic Auditorium
SEPTEMBER
1st Hollywood Florida Sportatorium
3rd New York Madison Square Gardens
4th Toronto Maple Leaf Gardens
5th Chicago Amphitheatre
7th Boston Gardens
9th Hampton Roads Coliseum
10th Syracuse Onadaga War Memorial
11th Rochester Memorial Auditorium
13th Berkeley Community Theatre
14th Berkeley Community Theatre
16th Honolulu International Center
17th Honolulu International Center

After a catastrophic show in Milan on July 5th (where the audience were teargassed by the local police) and a couple of shows in Montreux Switzerland, the band set off to North America where they opened in Vancouver, British Columbia at the Pacific Coliseum. The shows consistently continued to feature *Stairway* and *Going To California* while *Black Dog* was dropped in and out of the set. *Rock and Roll* was used as an encore periodically, but *Misty Mountain Hop* was shelved until the second Japanese tour in October 1972.

After playing to enthusiastic sold-out houses all across the States they concluded the tour with two shows in Hawaii, en-route to their first Japanese appearances. One performance of *Stairway to Heaven* stuck in Page's mind: *"I remember we did it in Los Angeles and got a standing ovation at the end of it and they'd never heard it before, obviously because the album didn't come out for another four to six weeks. It was such a moment because we all know how difficult it is to hear a song for the first time from a group in concert and it really hit home. It was a really emotional moment. We knew it was really something. Apparently, Robert's made some statements to the effect that the song wasn't well received originally. That's not true! I think Robert would remember that"*

On arriving in Tokyo the band were greeted by enthusiastic reporters and fans. Once again the concerts were a triumph for them. The bootleg recordings that have survived reveal the audiences to be more reminiscent of a Beatles crowd. There are moments where Plant has to talk them down due to the incredible noise they are making. The band responded in kind with a string of lengthy and disciplined performances. *Black Dog* was reinstated into the set and played every night

JAPAN TOUR 1971
SEPTEMBER
23rd Tokyo Budokan Hall
24th Tokyo Budokan Hall
27th Hiroshima Shiei Taiikukan
28th Osaka Festival Hall
29th Osaka Festival Hall

but *Rock and Roll* was saved until the last song of the last night in Japan.

The band returned in triumph to the UK at the end of September and began a promotional tour for the album release. On November 11th they kicked off their second UK tour that year and this time they played in the bigger halls. The three songs that had been in the set for almost the entire year were retained and *Rock And Roll* was now thrown into the middle of the set.

WINTER UK TOUR 1971

NOVEMBER
11th Newcastle City Hall
12th Sunderland Locarno
13th Dundee Caird Hall
16th Ipswitch St Matthew's Baths
17th Birmingham Kinetic Circus
18th Sheffield University
20th Wembley Empire Pool
21st Wembley Empire Pool
23rd Preston Town Hall
24th Manchester Free Trade Hall
25th Leicester University
29th Liverpool University
30th Manchester Kings Hall

DECEMBER
2nd Bournemouth Starkers
9th Coventry Locarno
21st Salisbury City Hall

THE SONGS

Black Dog

First known live performance:
Belfast Ulster Hall March 5th 1971
Last known live performance by Led Zeppelin:
London December 10th 2007
Video footage:
The motion picture The Song Remains The Same
Memorable bootleg version:
BBC In Concert April 1st 1971
Recorded at Headley Grange
Mixed at Island Studio One

Track one, side one, begins with what sounds like Page scrubbing the strings on his guitar leading into the unforgettable vocal intro. "Hey Hey Momma...", belts Plant, and then the band storms in with one of the great turn-around riffs in the Zep repertoire. The apparent simplicity of the track disguises its birth as a real team effort. Worked up in a rehearsal session the main riff came from John Paul Jones, but the complexities and turn-arounds and the other member's respective contributions were recorded for posterity. The bootleg CD **Stairway Sessions** includes two takes which deliver six minutes and fifty seconds of remarkable insight into the joint creative process involved in the creation of this rock anthem. Although clearly Jones' riff is the anchor to which the final song is tied, there are many moments when Page can be heard usurping the riff and turning it around to deliver the familiar links to the bridge. On at least one occasion John Bonham can be heard leading the trio into a break with an idea that made it into the final song. While this musical repartee is taking place, Plant can be heard concocting the lyrics on the spot with perhaps ten vocal verses (or interludes). The rehearsal reveals Plant singing a rough version of the now familiar call and response section that has remained an audience favourite to this day, "Ah Ah...Ah Ah...". This seems to have developed accidentally, as an ad lib, while the band found their way around the break.

In the final minute of the rehearsal Page can be heard delivering the lead over a Jones/Bonham rhythm very similar to the final take. When the track was recorded onto tape in its final form most of these elements survived from this early rehearsal.

Page: " That's the guitars warming up (during the intro). Whenever we got together from the third, fourth, fifth album etc., around that time we would always say 'what have you got?' to anybody else to see if Jonesy had anything. Robert and I were doing all of the writing up to that point, unless it was a number like a blues number.

For instance, "When the Levee Breaks"

and then we would make a split between the four of us. We were always trying to encourage Jonesy to come up with bits and pieces so to speak, cause that's usually what they were, he never came up with a complete whole song or anything, (until 'In Through the Out Door'), but he had this great riff with "Black Dog" and I added some sections to it as well and then we had the idea... actually I suggested, how you get the breaks with the vocals. That's it, I've finally owned up, as no one else will in the band, but that was the idea to give it the vocal thing then the riffs come in. I guess if you want to say that we leaned on something as far as the structure of it, you remember "Oh Well" by Fleetwood Mac, where it stops and there's a vocal, so there you are... now they'll sue us! The whole thing was to have a really heavy riff."

Plant: *"They're really attuned to all those time skips. These things aren't intentional, just little whims which we'll no doubt expand on the next album. When they're doing these kind of time skip riffs, Jimmy, John, and Bonzo suddenly come up with something like the passage on 'Black Dog'; play it, fall about all over the floor for ten minutes in fits of laughter; play it again, burst into laughter, then preserve it on tape."*

The guitar parts were created by four different tracks of Page's Les Paul. **Andy Johns** later commented about the sound. *"That was a trick I learned from Bill Hawelson, who worked* with Buffalo Springfield. We plugged Jimmy's sun-burst Paul into a direct box, and from there into a mike channel. I used the mike amp of the mixing board to get distortion. Then we put two 1176 Universal compressors in a series on that sound, and distorted the shit out of it and compressed it to hell. So that's two compressors in a row and we're cranking them like crazy. The only problem with that was, the second Jimmy would stop play-ing, a huge amount of background noise would come surging up, which we had to try and fix in the mix. It took an hour to get that to sound right, and I recall triple-tracking the riff with it. The thing that pleased me about that sound was that it was very efficient; easy to control. Suppose you were look-ing at the mixer, and all the other faders were halfway up. Well, by recording guitars in that fash-ion, you only needed to keep the faders a third of the way up. At the time, I thought it was damn fine and a novel effect. I listen to it now and find it kind of thin. We attempted to do that with other songs, but it didn't work out."

The nature of the song inspired **John Paul Jones** to comment: *"It was like a race to see who could finish first!"* The title of the song came from a fairly innocuous source.

Page: *"In this house, Headley Grange, there was an old Black Dog...it was really quite old and one night it had been off doing the things that dogs do, and then came back and slept all day. It was quite a powerful image at the time (laughs) so* *we called it Black Dog."*

Fig. 21

   As outlined in the previous chapters the song almost immediately became a crowd favourite and was performed live from its inception right up until the band's dissolution in 1980. Although it was included in every performance during the 1973 tour of the USA and it was included in the motion picture **"The Song Remains The Same"** it was dropped from the soundtrack album and therefore no live version was officially released other than on the videotape until the *BBC Sessions* album in 1997. (Fig.21) In 1975 the band had grown tired of trotting out the obligatory performance of *Whole Lotta Love* and so they used it as a brief intro to *Black Dog* during their encore. In 1977 it was dropped from the set list but it was re-instated at their show in Copenhagen on **July 23rd 1979**. During the 1980 tour of Europe *Black Dog* was introduced each night by Page who, not known for speaking on stage, surprised the fans by introducing it in the appropriate local language. Live versions also appeared on the remastered movie soundtrack in 2007, the official 2003 *DVD* and the 1972 live album *How The West Was Won*. It became the focal point of the media attention immediately after the 2007 reunion show in London.

Rock And Roll

First known live performance:
Copenhagen K.B. Hallen May 5th 1971
Last known live performance by Led Zeppelin:
London December 10th 2007
Video footage:
The motion picture The Song Remains The Same
Memorable bootleg version: Los Angeles June 23rd 1977
Recorded at Headley Grange
Mixed at Island Studio One and Olympic Studio

Track two, side one, begins with John Bonham thrashing out the intro to Little Richard's *Keep A Knockin'.* The rest of the song virtually fell together with Page and Jones bashing out some standard riffs.

Page: *"We had the drums in the hall and sometimes the drums were in the room as well, (in the sitting room with the fire place) and the amplifiers were all over. When Bonzo was in the hall, Jones and I were out there with earphones, the two sets of amps were in the other rooms and other places such as cupboards and things. A very odd way of recording but it certainly worked. When you've got the whole live creative process going on, that's how things like "Rock and Roll" come out.*

"I think we were attempting "Four Sticks" and it wasn't happening and Bonzo started the drum intro to "Keep a Knocking" (by Little

Richard) while the tape was still running and I played the riff automatically, that was "Rock and Roll" and we got through the whole first verse. We said this is great, forget "Four Sticks" let's work on this and things were coming out like that. (It) was a spontaneous combustion. It actually ground to a halt after about twelve bars, but it was enough to know that there was enough there as a number to keep working on it. Robert even came in singing on it straight away."

To flesh out the sound of the song it was decided that it needed piano. Ian Stewart was the obvious choice.

Andy Johns: "That was Stu. We were using the Stones mobile truck and he was the Stones roadie. They gave the truck to Stu to manage and he made some extra money. You know it was a perk. Jimmy knew Stu from when they were young, they were both from Epsom. They all knew Stu was the only guy in England to play that boogie thing authentically and there he was, so he played on it. That one was recorded at Headley it just happened."

Peter Green's Fleetwood Mac were certainly a powerful influence on Zeppelin. They may even have been living in Headley around the same time. Perhaps not coincidentally Fleetwood Mac also included Little Richard's "Keep A Knocking'" in their live set in the summer of 1970. Their arrangement is uncannily similar to

Zeppelin's Rock And Roll. It seems highly unlikely that Zeppelin would include a remake of "Keep A Knocking" as well as use the idea for "Oh Well" when they constructed Black Dog, without their being some indirect influence from the Fleetwood camp.

Rock and Roll was soon moved to the forefront of the Led Zeppelin pantheon. It was the opening number for the 1972 tours of Japan and the UK, the 1973 tours of Europe and the USA and the 1975 tour of the USA and Canada. In 1977 it was slotted into a medley with Whole Lotta Love as an encore and on one memorable occasion at the L.A. Forum Keith Moon joined in and played along with John Bonham for an explosive and hilarious version. Live versions appeared in 2003 on *How The West Was Won* (from 1972) (Fig 22) and the official *DVD* (from 1979). It was used as the final encore at the 2007 London reunion show.

Fig. 22

The Battle Of Evermore

First known live performance:
Dallas Memorial Auditorium April 1st 1977
Last known live performance by Led Zeppelin:
Oakland Coliseum July 24th 1977
Video footage: Plant & Page MTV Unledded TV Special
Memorable bootleg version: Los Angeles June 21st 1977
Recorded at Island Studio & Headley Grange
Mixed at Olympic Studios

Track three, side one, was a classic example of a Plant/Page collaboration. *The Battle Of Evermore* is composed from a Page mandolin structure and some notable Tolkienesque lyrics from Plant. As on "Ramble On" Plant dug into Tolkien's remarkable novel "The Lord Of The Rings" for his inspiration, although this time it seems as if the lyrics take the listener right into the novel. With Dark Riders and desperate heroes, it paints colorful audio images of battlefields and great quests. Tolkien himself had written songs for his novel which he had asked Donald Swann (half of the British composing duo **Flanders and Swann**) to put to music.

Donald Swann: *"(The Battle Of Evermore is)...the best example of a contemporary song based on Tolkien's work I've heard."*

The song began at Headley Grange when Page found a mandolin lying around one night.

Page: *"I remember seeing it. It wasn't mine, it was Jonesy's. We were living in the house, they would go to bed and I would sit up and play quite a bit... I just picked it up, got the chords, and it sort of started happening. I did it more or less straight off! I had never played one before, the tuning is totally different. It was my first experiment with a mandolin. I suppose all man-dolin players would have a great laugh, 'cos it must be the standard thing to play those chords, you know, but possibly not that approach. Anyway, it was just one of those things where I was governed by the limitations of the instrument. Possibly, afterwards, it sounded like a dance-around-the-maypole number I must admit, but it wasn't purposely like that 'Let's do a folksy num-ber'. There was something about that period... It was a time of great inspiration, you know."*

One of the most unusual aspects of the song was the appearance of a new vocalist for the first time on a Led Zeppelin record. **Sandy Denny** was known around Britain for her performances with Fairport Convention and The Strawbs. Her folky style blended perfectly with Plant's to provide the contrasts in the lyrics.

Page: *"Robert had this idea to bring in Sandy Denny. I thought it worked out well."*

There is some indication that Plant may have played guitar on the song.

Page: *"On "Battle of Evermore", he sings with Sandy Denny. Robert wrote the lyrics again for this album, but now he's getting more into playing the guitar himself, and he also plays drums, he finds that bits of melodies and riffs are also coming to him. Robert still hasn't plucked up the courage to play guitar on stage, but he is progressing well and he plays on the Sandy Denny track."*

Plant: *"A lot of tracks on that album came from various moods where we just got together and started to contribute to various basic ideas. If we roll up somewhere with amplifiers and guitars then there's electric music. If we roll up to my farm with acoustic guitars, that's something else and that's when the acoustic stuff gets written. In the case of one song, 'Battle of Evermore', I had been reading a book on the Scottish wars immediately before. It was really more of a playlet rather than a song and after I wrote the lyrics, I realized I needed a completely different voice as well as my own. So I asked Sandy Denny along to sing on that track. I found it very satisfying to sing with someone who has a completely different style to my own. While I sang about the events of the song, Sandy answered back as if she was the pulse of the people in the battlements. Sandy was the town crier, urging the people to lay down their weapons."*

Andy Johns remembered the session.

Johns: *"That was Island. Sandy was singing at the same time as Robert. I think the*

Mandolin was done at Headley Grange we used a Binson echo on the mandolin. It was one of these old Italian echo units with like a metal drum inside. We also used it on the drums on Levee."

Because of the obvious absence of Sandy Denny the band did not attempt to perform the song live until many years later. It was introduced into the set in 1977 and John Paul Jones was given the task of providing the vocal accompaniment. It also gave Jones a chance to show off his new triple neck guitar that featured, amongst other things, a mandolin. Although the bootlegs do not reveal the performances to be particularly impressive the audiences clearly loved the inclusion of the song. When Plant and Page reunited for their *No Quarter* project in 1994 (Fig 23) Battle Of Evermore was re-done with Najma Akhtar, a new talent, putting a different twist on the original arrangement to great effect. In 2007 Plant would record with Bluegrass singer Alison Krauss. Their album *Raising Sand* had many echoes of his work with Denny from 37 years earlier. Plant would perform the song with Krauss during his 2008 tour.

Fig. 23

Stairway To Heaven

First known live performance:
Belfast Ulster Hall March 5th 1971
Last known live performance by Led Zeppelin:
London December 10th 2007
Video footage: The official DVD
Memorable bootleg version:
Headley Grange December 1970 Rehearsal
Recorded at Island Studio One
Mixed at Island Studio One

Track four, side one. The most requested song in commercial radio history. Robert Plant himself had sworn to never sing it again due to its inordinate popularity, while radio programmers crack jokes about it and then play it again! It has transcended the realms of a simple pop song to enter the lexicon of everyday life. In *Wayne's World,* a hugely popular motion picture, the protagonist picks out the introductory notes of the song only to be reprimanded for breaking a policy against playing it. The lyrics have been dissected forwards and backwards by everyone, from curious fans, to right-wing religious zealots. In 1995 it was the subject of an entire CD full of parody versions, with everything from one-eyed pirates playing their wooden legs to Elvis impersonators. Reviled and adored, the song has a checkered history belying its relatively simple nature.

The band rehearsed the song at length at Headley Grange. In an interview in the 1970's John Bonham was asked whether the band had complete structures ready before they went into the studio.

John Bonham: *"No. The only thing that was at all like that was Stairway To Heaven. It had a rough outline to it before we started on it. Jimmy had a rough idea, but even that changed. That was the closest to what you just said though. 'Stairway To Heavens' are few and far between. Sometimes Jimmy does them before. Usually we put the backing track down and all the time we're recording Robert'll be sitting there writing vocals as we go along, then he'll take the backing track home and work on it. But he's always there - he's got to be, I suppose, to get any inspiration at all for it."*

Over the years Page has been the song's most vocal advocate. When Plant refused to perform the song again, after the band's demise, Page played it as an instrumental. His appearances during a string of charity concerts in 1983-1984 were highly charged emotional events with Stairway concluding the evenings' proceedings. Plant's absence was barely noticed as the audiences cheerfully sang along.

Page: *Bonzo and Robert had gone out for the night, and I worked really hard on the thing. Jonesy and I then routined it together. Later, we*

ran through it with the drums..Robert was sitting
there by the fireplace just writing away and suddenly there it was... It is a pretty good representation of what we are doing now. There are different moods in the song which lasts ten minutes.
We want to do a really long track one day, but not
yet. We know where we are going as a group. We
are four individuals who have found a common
denominator in music. There is a lot of inspiration
coming through on this new album. We're getting
better all the time. Robert's words to Stairway To
Heaven are brilliant - the best he's ever written. I
did write lyrics, but after Robert had written
'Stairway', there was just no point in my writing
any more lyrics since I wasn't gonna top anything
like that and he obviously was.

    "That number gave us the musical
respectability we deserved all along. It was put
together in such a way as to bring in all the fine
points musically of the band. Atlantic were desperate for us to put it out as a single, but I thought
it was wrong because there was the continuity in
the album that would have been broken, and with
this sort of music, the whole thing is to get as
much 'level' as you can, so the record sounds as
good on any kind of player. If the level is down,
you may lose a lot of bass sound. You have to
check all that in the cutting stages and in quality
control. I thought 'Stairway' crystallized the
essence of the band. It had everything there and
showed the band at its best . . . as a band, as a
unit. Not talking about solos or anything, it had

everything there. It was a milestone for us. Every musician wants to do something of lasting quality, something that will hold up for a long time and I guess we did it with 'Stairway'. Townshend probably thought that he got it with 'Tommy'. I don't know whether I have the ability to come up with more. I have to do a lot of hard work before I can get anywhere near those stages of consistent, total brilliance."

Plant: "*It was done very quickly. It was a very fluid unnaturally easy track. There was something pushing it saying 'you guys are OK, but if you want to do something timeless, here's a wedding song for you."*

When asked about the songs enormous popularity Plant is not at a loss for words.

"I think it was the ambiguity of the lyrics. Everybody can interpret them however they will. It's potential optimism, lyrically it's saying that if you hold tight, you can make it all right. Whatever it is, it's saying a different thing to every other person, as was Kashmir. It's also incredibly English. It sounds almost medieval. At times it sounds like, you know, you want to have swirling mists. I just know that there's so many different twists and turns to everyone's life. If you keep a diary or you express yourself in any way you refer to it. Writing songs kind of tells you how you were at the time at least how you were projecting yourself at various points in time.

"Jimmy and I just sat by the fire it was a remarkable setting, I mean Hawkwind were probably humming in the background! I don't consider there was anything particularly special about it. The only thing that gives it any staying power at all is its ambiguity. It's a very positive song. There's one very well known line "there's a lady who's sure all that glitters is gold," it's as old as the hills. From that moment on from writing that down "there's a lady who's sure all that glitters is gold"...she's going to get exactly what she wants..."and when she gets there she knows if the stores are all closed"...it's like she can have anything forever so long as she doesn't have to think about it... and so on... but good will prevail over the whole thing and logic will reign and all that. Jimmy and I just sat down in front of the fire and came up with a song which was later developed by the rest of the band in the studio."

Page: "I'd been fooling around with the acoustic guitar, and came up with different sections, which I married together. But what I wanted was something that would have the drums come in at the middle, and then we'd build to a huge crescendo. Also, I wanted it to speed up, which is against all musical...I mean, that's what a musician doesn't do, you see? So I had all the structure of it, and I ran it by John Paul Jones so he could get the idea of it—John Bonham and Robert had gone out for the night—and then on the following day we got into it with John Bonham. You have to realize that at first there was a hell of a lot for everyone to remember on this one. But as we were sort of routining it, Robert was writing down these lyrics, and a huge percentage of the lyrics were written there and then."

Andy Johns: I remember saying to Jimmy that I wanted to work on a song that started off real quiet and got bigger and bigger. And Pagey said, "Oh, don't worry, I've got one of those for this album. Wait till you hear it!" So I said, "Super." Jimmy had the tune pretty much worked out; I don't even recall hearing a demo. On the tracking, when we got around to doing the song, I could tell it was going to be special. Jimmy played acoustic in an iso booth. He was the thread that held it all together he played acoustic throughout. We had Bonzo out in the main room at the drums, and John Paul Jones was playing a Hohner electric."

Page: "It may not make a lot of sense but it was quite a complicated song to actually get across to everybody. I know one of the bits that was difficult for Bonzo at the time was the twelve string fanfare into the guitar solo and that took a bit of time. We were going over and over it from the beginning to the end quite a few times, with Robert sitting on the stool listening and he must have got inspiration as he wrote these lyrics then. He said I think I've got some things for it. We had an old Revox tape recorder at that time and I remember there were a good 70 to 80% of the lyrics there. There's actually a first rehearsal tape *of it, and sixty per cent of the lyrics Robert came in with off the cuff, which was quite something. When we were recording it, there were little bits, little sections that I'd done, getting reference pieces down on cassette, and sometimes I referred back to them if I felt there was something right that could be included. The song built towards a big climax with John Bonham coming in half-way through the song. It was an idea I'd used before, to give that extra kick. Then there's a fanfare towards the solo, and Robert comes in with a tremendous vocal."*

Page admitted later that the opening of Stairway was inspired by a comment from **George Harrison.** *"Bonzo told me he met George Harrison and he said that the problem with your band is that you don't do any ballads. So I purposely stuck the first two notes on of "Something". Stairway was just a number of different chord sequences and approaches that I'd worked on over a particular week and then it's like a paste up and slotting them all together 'til they work."*

Interestingly, Page makes no reference to the song *Taurus* by the band Spirit. Many critics in recent years have drawn attention to Stairway's uncanny similarities to the 1968 instrumental by guitar legend Randy California.

Zeppelin would relocate to Island Studios in London. Recording took place on an unspecified night in January 1971. Island Studios has now moved to another location, but the main room at the Basing Street location was apparently quite large. It was normal procedure to have one or more assistants on hand for setting up equipment and to generally provide an extra set of hands. On this particular night a young engineer called Richard Digby Smith pulled the shift.

Richard Digby Smith: *"There were about 4 or 5 assistants on the album. I just happened to be there that night. It was recorded at Island Basing Street Studio One. I was very young and to be able to get the luck that put me in there with musicians of that calibre was really something."*

John Paul Jones' recorder part that follows the delicate finger picking guitar intro had been the source of speculation for years. There were rumours that the part was played by Jones on mellotron or even synthesiser.

Page: *"Usually we could tackle anything between the four of us. Jonesy was such a multi instrumentalist, anyway... for instance he's doing the recorder part at the beginning of "Stairway". He is a brilliant musician."*

Andy Johns: *"That was real recorders Baritone, Tenor, Soprano I suppose maybe there were four or five tracks if I listened to it I would remember. That was done at Island it was Jonesy playing them all."*

The specific layout of the session was recalled in detail by Smith. His recollections indicate that the recorders were overdubbed at a later time and that Jones played keyboards for the bed tracks.

Richard Digby Smith: *"I can recall the take of Stairway to Heaven. It was a very large room. Page was playing acoustic guitar sat at the front with four tall baffles that completely enclosed him. There were no windows at all and you couldn't see in or out, it was just like a little square. Jones was to the right of him playing Moog bass which was the industry standard at the time. You know, it was a keyboard, Moog keyboard bass. Bonzo just sat at the back waiting for that bit where he comes pounding in, which is about ten minutes into the song (laughs). The first take was a good take and so they all came into the booth to listen. They always played everything back incredibly loud. Andy called it "Hooligan level". Anyway they were really pleased and it was an amazing take. So Bonzo put down his sticks and put his coat on and said, "That's that one nailed then." But Page was the only one who wasn't happy and he asked for another take. So the rest, who were mildly incensed, reluctantly went back into the studio. Bonham grabbed his sticks and said to Page, "You always do this to us, Jimmy!" So he stormed back into the room and sat down there with steam coming out of his ears and it was quite tense! Then they did another take and that was the one. When we heard it back it was much better. Bonham just* *looked at Page and said something like, "You Bastard! You were right." and Page said, "Yeah, that's what I wanted."*

After completing the bed track in only two takes the next job was the overdubs. Although there are few specifics in anyone's recollections about the vocal and recorder parts, Page has been interviewed multiple times about the now legendary guitar solo. In one interview he was asked whether he had demoed the solo but he stated that although he had not worked out the notes he had spent some time working on the orchestration.

Page: *"I winged it (the solo) every time... the slide bits, that's orchestration. I had prepared the overall structure of the guitar parts but not the actual notes. I did have the first phrase worked out, and then there was the link phrase. But when it came time to record the solo I warmed up and did three of them. They were all quite different from each other. I did check them out beforehand, before the tape ran. The one we used was the best solo, I can tell you that. That's how I did all of 'em. I tinkered about with the amps to get a sound. But by the time I'd reached the solo I'd already put all the other guitar overlays on. In most of the songs the solos were the last things to be done, near enough. I'd do the guitar overlays, and then Robert would come in and carry on with the vocals. Invariably, I'd put the guitar solo on last. Unless it was something I did live."*

Many people to this day think that Page used his trademark double neck Gibson to record Stairway.

Page: *"I didn't use a double-neck on that, but I had to get one afterwards to play it. I did all those guitars on it; I just built them up. That was the beginning of my building up harmonized guitars properly. I know everyone knows me for the double neck, but in fact I had to get the double neck to handle "Stairway" live, because even though I had played six string acoustic, electric and twelve string electric. I couldn't do it on one or the other. The double neck was the only way of being able to handle it. The main thing is, there's an effect you can get where you leave the 12-string neck open as far as the sound goes and play the 6-string neck and you get the 12-strings vibrating in sympathy. It's like an Indian sitar, and I've worked on that a little bit. I use it on "Stairway" like that; not on the album but on the soundtrack and film. It's surprising; it doesn't vibrate as heavily as a sitar would, but nonetheless it does add to the overall tonal quality."*

In several interviews Page claimed he couldn't recall which guitar and amp he used for the solo, at one point suggesting that it might have been a Marshall, but finally in the 1990's he revealed the answer.

Page: *"That solo was done on the Tele, interestingly enough, I'd returned to the*

Telecaster. I was just getting too much feedback. I steered away from the Les Paul because it was all sort of there giving it all to you, the sustain and stuff.... The "Stairway to Heaven" solo was done when I pulled out the Telecaster which I hadn't used for a long time, plugged it into the Supro, and away it went again. That's a different sound entirely from any of the first album. It was a good versatile setup."

Once more Smith recalls the details.

Richard Digby Smith: *"Page did three takes of the guitar solo. I was sitting next to Andy when we played all three back. It was a toss up between the second and third takes. I had heard one bit in the third take which I liked and I was anxious to put my two pennies worth in so I said they should use that bit of take three and Andy looked at me and asked if I wanted to sit in his chair! I think they may have used that bit although I wouldn't know what bit it was anymore. Every time I hear that solo I can still see Page playing it. It was stunning. It was a really big room, which they liked because they could get that big drum sound. We did a lot of orchestral stuff in there. Now, orchestral musicians don't like using headphones much so we had these big Tannoy monitors which we would wheel in for the orchestras and bolt to the floor. So Page used these things for the solos. There were these big orange speakers with Page standing between them and we played him back through them as loud as possible and he just leaned up against the speakers with his ear virtu-*

ally pressed against them with a cigarette hanging out of his mouth and rattled out that solo."

When the song was finally recorded the mixdown was done at Island by Andy Johns. One lucky journalist was on hand for the occasion.

Review: *"The first time I heard STAIRWAY TO HEAVEN during a mix-down session at Island it made a lasting impression on me. For my money this is Zeppelin's all time classic and undoubtedly one of the finest tracks by any group this year. Plant's phrasing is superb, placing sympathetic emphasis on the lyrics and proving that his forte is not reserved for lung busting belters. The tune builds slowly and very softly with acoustic guitars and what I believe to be recorders. As the ethereal mood builds the sound is augmented with electric instruments yet in no way does it destroy the mood which prevails throughout. This track alone is worth the price of the album."*

In the 1980's attention was drawn to the song because it had become the most requested song in American radio history. At one point it had reputedly racked up an impressive one million plus plays. One of the downsides to this unprecedented popularity is the inevitable increase in criticism. The band suddenly found themselves to be the target of a crusade by several lunatic religious groups who claimed that the song was some kind of satanic verse. The fact that one faction of the **O.T.O**. (an organisation which Aleister Crowley founded) stated that it was Page's ultimate satanic song, aggravated an already ludicrous situation. Immediately the fringe fanatics of middle America threw every accusation they could at the band, suggesting that because Page had an interest in occult books and because Led Zeppelin had been plagued with bad luck combined with enormous financial success, then they must surely be satanists. At one point some bright spark suggested playing Stairway To Heaven backwards because there was a secret satanic message in the lyrics. The pure idiocy of these claims did not escape the band who generally shrugged them off.

Page: *"I have heard it played backwards and it was quite amusing as opposed to amazing. Look, if I spent my life playing my whole record collection backwards while I was in my teens and trying to learn guitar, I would never have gotten where I did. It was like the whole thing about Paul is dead from the Beatles. It was just some guy with a sense of humor. It was quite possible it might work out that way in reverse - But it's positive and negative isn't it? Honestly, you should ask Robert because he did the lyrics, Yet all this stuff is always aimed at me. I mean, you figure they're listening to an 8 1/2 minute song. They're listening to all the lyrics, they could find one that sounds like something in reverse. The whole situation's a joke. It's stupid people. They try to advertise the fact that they've found some great key to something. They wouldn't understand the key if they even heard it in* *the first place. It's as simple as that, they don't know. Those records were extremely emotional and if that's the way they interpret it, if that deep intense emotion was satanic then, they've got no idea what we were about."*

They rehearsed the song for their upcoming tour of America in September of 1980 and then performed it at the two reunion events **Live Aid** and the **Atlantic Records 40th** anniversary party, but the last time that *Led Zeppelin* would perform the song in concert would be a memorable occasion. At the **Berlin Eissporthalle** on **July 7th 1980** they played what was destined to be their last concert as Led Zeppelin. Although the band had no way of knowing that it would be their last show, they turned in a startling version which is now known to be probably the longest version ever, clocking it at over fifteen minutes!

In the 1990's an Australian called **Rolf Harris**, who had been a hugely successful television entertainer in the UK in the sixties, released a version of Stairway To Heaven. It came replete with his own inimitable vocal stylings, digereedoos and wobble boards and shot straight to the top of the British singles chart. It was followed by an entire album of parodies of the song that sold well around the world. On a press tour of Australia in 1994 Plant and Page were subjected to several video performances of these parodies on Australian TV. Both took the jibes with good humour and Plant voiced his own appreciation of both Harris and the Elvis impersonator's versions. They concluded the interview with a rendition of Harris sixties hit "**Sun Arise**". On the same press tour they appeared on a late-night Japanese newscast for which they agreed they would take a request and perform it on the spot. The request, naturally, was Stairway which Plant had vowed he would never sing again. Right up until the cameras were ready to roll they were going to perform "Babe I'm Gonna Leave You," but at the last minute Plant relented and they performed a truncated, but surprisingly soulful version of Stairway, with just guitar and vocal. Rumour has it that Page was so surprised that he jokingly punched Plant after the cameras stopped rolling. To many people's surprise the band included it in their 2007 London reunion show. As of this writing this is the last known performance, making a fitting conclusion to the performing history of this unparalleled song. Phil Carson, who was VP of Atlantic records in the UK at the time, comments about the song's success.

Phil Carson: *"Once again, history proved that Peter Grant was right. There had already been two singles off the album, but Atlantic US wanted to revitalise the fourth album prior to the release of the new one, plus the upcoming tour. It was a natural enough move. A lot of AM stations did programme 'Stairway', but it didn't come out as a single . . . so people just bought the album as if it were a single. Which added at least 500,000 copies to the total sales of the album."*

Plant: *"It was a nice pleasant well-meaning naive little song, very English. It's not the definitive Led Zeppelin song. Kashmir is. I'd break out in hives if I had to sing Stairway To Heaven in every show. I wrote those lyrics and found that song to be of some importance and consequence in 1971, but 17 years later, I don't know. It's just not for me. I sang it at the Atlantic Records show because I'm an old softy and it was a way of saying thank you to Atlantic because I've been with them for 20 years. But no more of Stairway to Heaven for me."*

Jones: *"I actually like "Stairway." I know that's really corny. But it encompasses a lot of the elements of the band, from the acoustic start to the slightly jazzier section, even, and then to the heavier stuff towards the end. It was a very successful song. I'm not talking about it's being successful in commercial terms, but successful in that everything worked well and fell into place. Everything built nicely."*

Page: *"We knew it was good, we didn't realise that people would latch onto it. We thought that's great, fabulous."*

Richard Digby Smith: *"You'd never think people would be talking about this 25 years later I sometimes get people coming up to me saying, "I know someone who assisted on Stairway To Heaven", but I was the only assistant that night. I was very fortunate to be working with Andy. It* *gives me chills even now when I hear it because I can still see them doing that take. You know when you hear a piece of music and you were there, it sticks. I will never forget Bonzo doing that drum intro."*

Live versions of Stairway to Heaven appeared in 1997 on *BBC Sessions*, in 2003 on *How The West Was Won* (from 1972) and from Earl's Court 1975 on the official 2003 *DVD*.

Sheet Music

Misty Mountain Hop

First known live performance:
Copenhagen K.B. Hallen May 3rd 1971
Last known live performance by Led Zeppelin:
London December 10th 2007
Video footage:
The movie The Song Remains The Same remastered 2007
Memorable bootleg version:
Tokyo Budokan Hall October 2nd 1972
Recorded at Headley Grange
Mixed at Olympic Studios

Track one, side two. Misty Mountain Hop has become one of Robert Plant's favourite Led Zeppelin tracks. Originally conceived during rehearsal at Headley Grange, not much is known about the song or how it came about. It was first performed at the concert in Copenhagen on May 5th 1971. Unfortunately, the performance was less than memorable, with the band losing their place multiple times. Along with Four Sticks it was promptly dropped from the live set and was not resurrected for eighteen months. Its subsequent performances on the band's second successful tour of Japan, clearly etched the song firmly into the Zep pantheon as a good song for getting the audience on their feet. As late as the Atlantic reunion party in 1988 and again at the Silver Clef Award Winners concert at Knebworth in 1990, Plant was clearly happy to include the song in the set.

Plant: *"It's about a bunch of hippies getting busted... about the problems you can come across* *when you have simple walk in the park on a nice sunny afternoon. In England it's understandable because wherever you go to enjoy yourself 'Big Brother' is not far behind. Big Brother being the paranoiac establishment."*

Apparently there had been a bust some-where near London where a group of people were arrested for possession of marijuana. By 1973 Misty Mountain Hop was firmly entrenched in the live set and was being used as a lead-in to *Since I've Been Loving You*. Unfortunately it was dropped from the motion picture and so for years we only saw the guitar break into the next song. This was rectified for the 2003 *DVD* and the 2007 remaster-ing of the movie. The title once again reflects Plant's preoccupation with Tolkien and his Lord Of The Rings trilogy. The title comes from the name of the mountain range in Tolkien's fictional Middle Earth. Basic recording was done at Headley Grange using the Rolling Stones Mobile studio and the mixdown was done by Andy Johns at Olympic Studios.

Page: *"I remember "Misty Mountain Hop" - I remember coming up with the opening part of that and then we would go off into that. Jonesy put the chords in for the chorus bit and that would shape up. We used to work pretty fast. A lot of that song would have been made up during the point of being at Headley."*

Plant: *"It's a song for anyone who ever got waylaid when they were going somewhere."*

Four Sticks

First known live performance:
Copenhagen K.B. Hallen May 3rd 1971
Last live performance by Led Zeppelin:
Copenhagen K.B. Hallen May 3rd 1971
Video footage: Plant & Page Unledded MTV Special
Memorable bootleg version:
Copenhagen K.B. Hallen May 3rd 1971
Recorded at Island Studios
Mixed at Olympic Studios

Track two, side two. Once again the rehearsal for this began at Headley Grange. The song title came from Bonham picking up four drum sticks, out of frustration, and playing it with both sets in his hands.

Page: *""Four Sticks", I remember, we tried that on numerous occasions and it didn't come off until the day Bonzo... who was just playing with two sticks on it... picked up two sets of sticks, and we did it. That was two takes, but that was because it was physically impossible for him to do another. I couldn't get that to work until we tried to record it a few times and I just didn't know what it was and I still wouldn't have known what it was, we probably would have kicked the track out, but then Bonzo went and... I'm not going to repeat the language he said at the time, but it was nothing to do with the fact that it was taking a long time. We had actually gone in to try on a fresh occasion and he just picked up the four sticks, and that was it. So in fact purely because of that the whole* *thing changed really. It was really abstract. It was supposed to be abstract. I think it is too, you know lyrically as well. We tried different ways of approaching it, then we had a Double Diamond, picked up four sticks and did it again, and it was magic, one take, and the whole thing had suddenly been made."*

Bonham: *""With a certain amount of the songs, Jimmy'll come in with the chords to it, and then we'll work on it. Somebody might come up with an idea for a middle or a different section, but he'll have done the basics. The other thing that happens is if somebody comes up with a riff, and then we'll work on it to make it into a song."*

Page was experimenting with different sounds at this time which involved using different amps and different ways of recording.

Page: *""Four Sticks" in the middle section of that. The sound of those guitars; that's where I'm going. I've got really long pieces written; I've got one really long one written that's harder to play than anything. It's sort of classical, but then it goes through changes from that mood to really laid-back rock, and then to really intensified stuff. I could get a lot of tones out of the guitar which you normally couldn't. This confusion goes back to those early sessions again with the Les Paul. Those might not sound like a Les Paul, but that's what I used. It's just different amps, mike placings, and all different things. Also, if you just crank it up* *to distortion point so you can sustain notes, it's bound to sound like a Les Paul. I was using the Supro amp for the first album and still do."*

The full sound and hypnotic feel of the song were once again Jones handiwork.

Andy Johns: *"That was a moog synthesiser. It was done at Island, that was Jonesy again."*

Four Sticks was performed only once by Led Zeppelin, and although the performance was a memorable one, it was not revived until Plant and Page's remarkable version in 1994 with a full orchestra. As such it is one of the more obscure moments in the Zeppelin catalogue.

After touring Australia in February 1972 Plant and Page decided to make their way home via Bombay India. This detour became an important moment in the band's history due to a remarkable recording session that took place in the first week of March with the Bombay Symphony Orchestra. An astonishingly good bootleg recording exists of them attempting versions of Four Sticks and Friends. It is not too hard to see the similarities between this session and what emerged 22 years later on the Unledded album.

At one point this song contributed to the strings of delays that plagued the release of the album when the master tape went missing.

Going To California

First known live performance:
Belfast Ulster Hall March 5th 1971
Last live performance by Led Zeppelin:
Oakland County Coliseum July 24th 1977
Video footage: The official *DVD* (Earl's Court 1975)
Memorable bootleg version:
BBC In Concert April 1st 1971
Recorded at Headley Grange
Mixed at Olympic Studios

Track three, side two. Inspired by Robert Plant's affection for Canadian singer songwriter Joni Mitchell. Going to California was an immediate favourite at the band's concerts. Introduced for the first time in Belfast on March 5th 1971 the band then performed a near perfect performance for the BBC In Concert broadcast three weeks later. It was the first time that the British audiences had heard anything from the upcoming album. Although Page made claims that this song was originally conceived long before Led Zeppelin even was formed he seems to contradict himself in a later interview.

Page: *"That was another late night guitar twiddle, you know, the structure of it was done at Headley. That was the good thing about staying at that place. You didn't have anything like a snooker table or anything like that. No recreational distractions at all. It was really good for discipline* *and getting on with the job. I suppose that's why a lot of these things... for instance "Going to California" and "Battle of Evermore" came out. But obviously then we got together and it was just away. It was Jonesy on the mandolin, myself and Robert singing on it. We went over to mix it at Sunset Sound. This is Andy Johns and myself and Peter Grant was there as well. The funny thing is on "Going to California" you've got "The noises of the canyon got to tremble and shake" curiously enough when we landed, this is absolutely true. Apparently, as we were coming down the escalators into the main terminal there was a slight earthquake. In fact, it was quite big actually. It cracked one of the dams there in San Diego and in the hotel before going to the studio you could feel the bed shaking. I thought 'Well, here we go'."*

The interesting thing about this anecdote is that it pinpoints the exact date that Page and Johns arrived in Los Angeles for the mixdown. At 6 a.m. on the morning of February 9th an earthquake measuring 6.6 struck the San Fernando Valley and cracked one of the dams in the area. There were multiple large aftershocks, but this event along with Andy Johns statement that they worked for ten days pretty much puts the mixdown session as probably February 10th to the 20th or there-abouts. On returning to England the band were scheduled to begin the tour on March 5th and so the bad mix would have created something of a crisis. The next mix at Island and

Olympic would have been pushed back to perhaps April.

John Bonham: *"You know if you listen to all the albums you can say, "That sounds like Zeppelin" because it's a sound, you know. But in actual fact each album is very different. There's two tracks of acoustic (on the new album) Going To California, that's mandolin and acoustic guitar. It's just the songs that we write at a particular time and then we say, right we'll put them on an album. So the next one will probably be different still."*

Going To California became another of Plant's favourites and it was constantly moved in and out of the live set over the next few years. It became a permanent feature during the 1971 tours, was then dropped for a couple of years before being revived for the band's string of dates at Earl's Court in London in 1975. It then survived throughout the 1977 tour of the USA. Live versions appeared on *BBC Sessions*, *How The West Was Won* and the official *DVD*. (Fig 24)

Fig 24

When The Levee Breaks

First known live performance:
Brussels Vorst National January 12th 1975
Last known live performance by Led Zeppelin:
Chicago Stadium January 20th 1975
Video footage: Plant & Page MTV Unledded Special
Memorable bootleg version:
Chicago Stadium January 20th 1975
Recorded at Headley Grange
Mixed at Sound Sunset Studios

Track four, side two. The thunderous conclusion to the album begins with what can only be described as the most copied drum pattern in history. John Bonham's monumental intro has cropped up on everything from TV commercials to Rap records. When The Levee Breaks was originally written by **Memphis Minnie** in 1928 and was recorded by Minnie and Kansas Joe McCoy on February 21st 1930. The only identifiable part of the original is the lyric, as Page, Plant, Jones and Bonham unleash a thunderous, densely packed blues pattern that would have probably made Minnie cower in a corner. The backbone of the song is Bonham's drum sound which has been debated in great detail over the years and copied by every band who ever wanted to scare the neighbours. When asked, Page claimed it was one of the hardest tracks they ever did.

Page: *"Levee Breaks. We tried to record that in a studio before we got to Headley Grange, and it sounded flat. But once we got the drum sound at Headley Grange, it was like, boom, and that made the difference immediately. It was very exciting to listen to that drum sound on the head-phones. The idea was to bring in something new on every verse sometimes very subtle, maybe a change in the vocal texture and things like that."*

Page comments on the drum sound. *"The secret of a lot of this is the fact of where it was recorded. John Bonham was actually in the hallway of a three story house. He's in the hallway on his own and the stairwell is leading up all the way round and there's one stereo mike sticking out one and a half floors above the kit. There actually was a bass drum mike set up, but it didn't get used because we already had such a balance of the sound. So what you're hearing is the sound of the hall with the stereo mike on the stairs, second flight up. The rest of us were in another room except I had my amplifier in another room."*

Johns: *"The drums were done with two limiters one on each side we only used two mikes. They were up on the next floor landing or something like that."*

Page had spent many sessions in the stu-dio with some of the sixties greatest producers and he had observed all that could go wrong when trying to capture sound accurately

Page: *"It came from the session days really, and my own experience of having seen the Yardbirds being produced. Listening to the drums while playing next to them, and going to the control room and hearing what was coming back on the tape and realizing the drums were losing all their harmonics and depth. Wanting to try and rectify that is where the whole ambiance thing started.Having worked in the studios for so long as a session player, I had been on so many sessions where the drummer was stuck in a little booth and he would be hitting the drums for all he was worth and it would just sound as though he was hitting a cardboard box. I knew that drums would have to breathe to have that proper sound, to have that ambiance. So, consequently we were working on the ambiance of everything, of the instruments, all the way through. I guess this is the high point of this album. But that whole drum sound and all this ambiance is now captured digitally in the machine. Where we would do it that way, you have now got it in machines. I think we set a trend with all of this. Obviously, from the way we progressed, you can see how we got more adventurous. But the hallway is responsible for that one and "In My Time Of Dying." We did put a bit of echo on, but I guess I shouldn't say that!"*

Andy Johns: *"The tracks from Headley were R&R, Levee Breaks, & Boogie with Stu. The other guys were out having a drink, and John Bonham and I were at the house. He still com-*

plained that he wasn't getting the sound he wanted. Now, it always seemed to me that you couldn't get a proper sound out of drums by sticking mikes two inches away from them, so I finally said to him, "I've got an idea." We got his drums and put him in the hallway, and then hung two M 160 mikes from the staircase and pointed them towards the kit. His kit was very well-balanced internally, each drum's volume was consistent with the others. In the truck I put him into two channels and compressed the hell out of the drums. Jimmy had this Italian echo unit called a Binson that used a steel drum instead of a tape it had a really special sound and I used that as well. I remember sitting there thinking it sounded utterly amazing, so I ran out of the truck and said, "Bonzo, you gotta come in and hear this!" And he came in and shouted, "Whoa, that's it! That's what I've been hearing!" It's a technique I've used ever since: room mikes for the main drum sound, and then close-mikes mixed in."

Page: *"I believe, to the best of my recollection, that John Bonham had been attempting "Levee" before as a riff. I had a whole concept of how this thing was going to end up. That was it... it was going to be "THE" drum song. As soon as it was set up, it was the one we went for and it worked. We had a couple of attempts at it before which just didn't feel right. It must have been in the hands of the gods really. We would say 'wait until the drum kit arrived and everything is going to be fine'. At the end of it where we've got the* *whole works going on this fade, it doesn't actually fade, as we finished it the whole effects start to spiral, all the instruments are now spiralling. This was very difficult to do in those days. I can assure you. With the mixing and the voice remaining constant in the middle. This only really comes out on the headphones. You hear everything turning right around. In fact, at the time I was extremely happy with "The Levee".*

Another aspect of When The Levee Breaks is the sound that Page and Johns used for Plant's harmonica and Page's guitar. Both employed a technique called backwards echo. This involved running the tape backwards while processing it through an echo unit and then recording the resulting sound. When the tape is played forwards the echo seems to rush out ahead of the sound creating a bizarre and very powerful effect.

Johns: *"That was done at Island. I put the harp through an old Fender Princeton with tremolo and miked it up. It was Jimmy's idea to phase the vocal. We did the phasing when we mixed it afterwards."*

Page: *"It was backwards-echo harp. Actually, it could even be a backwards harp you know, a harp reversed around. But I actually invented that backwards echo, anyway. I know I did. It was on a Yardbirds track. There had already been backwards guitar bits, but I thought, "Why* *not have backwards echo?" The effect on 'When The Levee Breaks' is phased twelve strings on the riff but the fuzzy effect on the fade is a backward echoed Les Paul."*

Although When The Levee Breaks was not played very often it has become a classic of the Zeppelin arsenal. The first public performance was at one of the warm up shows for the American tour of 1975. It only lasted through two or three shows. It was not exhumed again until the Plant Page tour of 1994/95 when an entirely new version, more along the lines of the original Memphis Minnie song, was recorded for the duo's Unledded album. In a final comment about the song Robert Plant pays tribute to his friend.

Plant: *"It was a giant step. We got the most amazing drum sound and we played to it. It was an old tune but once the drums were miked up and we heard that sound, we had to submit. We could have played anything and it would have sounded good. Nobody other than John Bonham could have created that sex groove, and many have tried."*

FINAL COMMENTS

Bonham: *"My personal view is that the album is the best thing we've ever done. But that's strictly my personal view. I love it. It's the fourth album and it's the next stage we were in at the time of the recording. All the albums have been different and to my mind this is the best, and that's not trying to be big-headed, or flash. The playing is some of the best we've done and Jimmy is like ...mint!"*

Page agrees that the fourth album featured some of his best moments.

Page: *"Without a doubt. As far as inventiveness and as far as the quality of playing on the whole album, I would say yes. But I don't know what the best solo I've ever done is. I have no idea. My vocation is more in composition really than in anything else. Building up harmonies. Using the guitar, orchestrating the guitar like an army, a guitar army. I think that's where it's at really for me. I'm talking about actual orchestration in the same way you'd orchestrate a classical piece of music. Instead of using brass and violins you treat the guitars with synthesisers or other devices; give them different treatments, so that they have enough frequency range and scope and everything to keep the listener as totally committed to it as the player is. It's difficult. It's a difficult project, but it's one that I've got to do."*

Plant: *"A lot of the tracks on that album came from various moods where we just got together and started to contribute to various basic ideas. There's no yardstick for what we turn out. I'm 23 years old and I'm learning all the time, so that I look back to stuff I did two years ago and say, "Yeah, but I've gone on from there." Somebody said to me, "The second album was so good, whatever happened on the third?" What can you say? They didn't understand that you can't do 'Whole Lotta Love' eight times an album. Bonzo and I have the same idea that we should be playing at least twice a week. We started off as rock-n-rollers, so what else is there to do?"*

Would Page change anything on the record?

Page: *"Yes, I would do it with click tracks, synthesizers and sampling and then I would retire. No, no I've really got fond memories of those times and the album was done with such great spirit. Everyone had a smile on their faces. It was great. Purely for that reason, I would say 'No'."*

In January 2006 the RIAA declared that Led Zeppelin's ☉ ⚚ ⚘ ⊙ was the fourth best selling album of all time with total sales in excess of 23 million units in the United States.

In 2007 the band released *Mothership, a compilation album which included four tracks from* ☉ ⚚ ⚘ ⊙. The album was declared double platinum by the RIAA in February 2008.(Fig. 25)

ACKNOWLEDGEMENTS

The author wishes to *still* thank:

Andy Johns, Richard Digby Smith, Danny Coyle, Mike Kull, Brad Tolinski, Dave Lewis, Dayne & Pat Markham, Mark Robinson, Leo Ishaac, Chris Welch, Jo Broom & family, John Owen Smith, Ritchie Yorke, Brenda Poole & Winchester Local Studies Library, and McMaster University Library

And an extra special thank you to Duncan Watson who continues to steadily dig into the origins of Jimmy Page's symbol.

And to Mike Tremaglio for concert date corrections.

Fig. 25

BIBLIOGRAPHY

Led Zeppelin - Chris Welch Proteus 1984

Tight But Loose The Led Zeppelin Fanzine - Dave Lewis Bedford UK

Led Zeppelin The Press Reports - Robert Godwin 2004

The Led Zeppelin Biography - Ritchie Yorke Underwood Miller 1993

Guitar World - Brad Tolinski (Various issues)

Led Zeppelin Heaven & Hell - Charles Cross & Erik Flannigan Harmony 1991

Led Zeppelin Live - Luis Rey Hot Wacks 1993

The Illustrated Collector's Guide To Led Zeppelin - Robert Godwin CGP 1994

One Monday In November (The Headley Workhouse Riots of 1830) - John O. Smith

Rosicrucian Questions & Answers - H. Spencer Lewis 1928

The Rosicrucian Manual - H. Spencer Lewis

The Secret Doctrine - Helene Petrovna Blavatsky

Incidents In The Life Of Mme. Blavatsky - A.P. Sinnett 1866

The Magicians Of The Golden Dawn - Ellic Howe 1972

Timaeus And Critias - Plato

The Sacred Symbols Of Mu - James Churchward 1934

Dictionary Of Symbols - J.E. Cirlot

The Migration Of Symbols - Donald Mackenzie

The Book Of Signs - Rudolf Koch

Shepherd's Glossary Of Graphic Signs & Symbols - Walter Shepherd

The Book Of Signs & Symbols - I. Schwarz-Winklhofer & H. Biedermann

Secret Symbols Of The Rosicrucians - AMORC/H. Spencer Lewis 1616

The Triple Vocabulary Infernal Manual of Demonography or The Ruses of Hell Uncovered by Frinellan

Le véritable Dragon Rouge ou il est traité de l'art de commander les esprits infernaux by Anon

The Secret Book of Artephius by Artephius c. 12th century

Post - Led Zeppelin, Live In Montreux Switzerland October 1972.

Photograph courtesy Repfoto - Barrie Wentzell